THE EARLY
ARCHITECTURE
OF MADISON,
INDIANA

Shrewsbury house staircase   *Jack Boucher*

John T. Windle

Robert M. Taylor, Jr.

THE EARLY ARCHITECTURE OF MADISON, INDIANA

HISTORIC MADISON, INC.

INDIANA HISTORICAL SOCIETY

Madison and Indianapolis 1986

Madison and Indianapolis 1986

© 1986 Historic Madison, Inc., and the Indiana
Historical Society

Library of Congress Cataloging-in-Publication Data
Windle, John T., 1901–
   The early architecture of Madison, Indiana.

   Bibliography: p.
   Includes index.
   1. Greek revival (Architecture) — Indiana — Madison.
2. Architecture, Modern — 19th century — Indiana — Madison.
3. Architecture — Indiana — Madison. 4. Madison (Ind.) —
Buildings, structures, etc. I. Taylor, Robert M., 1941–
II. Title.
NA735.M32W46   1986   720′.9772′13   86-25653
ISBN 0-87195-004-9 (alk. paper)

The paper in this book meets the guidelines for permanence
and durability of the Committee on Production Guidelines
for Book Longevity of the Council on Library Resources.

Photographs credited HABS/HAER were produced by the
Historic American Buildings Survey/Historic American
Engineering Record, a division of the National Park Service,
United States Department of the Interior, Washington,
D.C. 20240. The function of HABS/HAER is to record
through photographs, architectural drawings, and historic
data, the significant and historic architectural and engineering
heritage of our country. These recordings are then transmit-
ted to the Library of Congress where they are preserved and
maintained. Inquiries can be made by writing to the Division
of Prints and Photographs, Library of Congress,
Washington, D.C. 20540.

Preface

A BOOK on the architecture of Madison, Indiana, is long overdue. Of the small cities in the Old Northwest Territory, Madison has probably the best collection of early and mid-nineteenth-century architecture surviving today.

This book was to have been written by the late Wilbur Peat, director of the John Herron Art Museum, some twenty years ago. Several years after our local preservation organization, Historic Madison, Inc., was founded and soon after his book, *Indiana Houses of the Nineteenth Century*, had been published by the Indiana Historical Society, Peat came to me with the idea of our collaborating on a book about early Madison architecture. Through his aegis Historic Madison received a grant from Lilly Endowment for the publication of the book. A further sum was added by a gift from the late Mrs. Walter Greiner. Peat made numerous trips to Madison, taking preliminary photographs of various structures and talking with me about the scope of the book. Then, tragically, in 1966, Wilbur Peat died.

The responsibility for doing the book was left to me. Through the ensuing years much research was done, and many photographs were collected. However, the task of building a strong organization for the purpose of preserving and restoring some of Madison's fine old buildings assumed first priority. Work on the book had to be set aside until Historic Madison, Inc., was established on a firm financial basis, allowing for a director and office manager. But by that time, completing the book alone had become an impossibility.

Then, in 1983, the Board of Trustees of the Indiana Historical Society, encouraged by its executive secretary, Gayle Thornbrough, came to the rescue. Not only did the Society supply me with an able member of its staff, Dr. Robert M. Taylor, Jr., as coauthor, to write the historical background of the subject and to assist in research, but it also offered to share in the costs of publication, which had risen sharply during the inflationary years. It is impossible to express adequately my gratitude to the members of the board of the Society. Without their generosity, this book could never have been published.

Of the many people to whom I am indebted in the writing of this book, the first is Wilbur Peat, who had the original idea and who largely planned its contents. Another is Rexford Newcomb, former dean of the School of Architecture at the University of Illinois. It was in Newcomb's classrooms as an undergraduate that my interest in architecture was born. Years later, after I had moved to Madison, he visited me and our friendship was renewed. He was at that time completing his book, *Architecture of the Old Northwest Territory*. In his preface he wrote, "There yet remains to be written a definitive monograph on the architecture of each of the six states of the Old Northwest." Peat's

Indiana Houses of the Nineteenth Century did just that for Indiana.

Many architects and architectural historians with a deep love for Madison have each in his own way inspired or encouraged me. I cannot fail to pay tribute to the late Lee Burns, author of *Early Architecture and Builders of Indiana*; the late Earl Reed, Midwest preservation officer for the National Trust for Historic Preservation; the late Edward D. James, national vice-chairman of the American Institute of Architects, Committee on Preservation; and H. Roll McLaughlin, F.A.I.A., a founder and former chairman of Historic Landmarks Foundation of Indiana.

I would like to express my deep appreciation to Howard E. Wooden, formerly the director of the Sheldon Swope Art Gallery in Terre Haute, Indiana, and presently director of the Wichita Art Museum, for his careful reading of the manuscript before publication. He did the same for Wilbur Peat's book some twenty-five years ago.

Robert Taylor's and my special thanks are due Anna Laura Peddie, former Jefferson County Recorder, for her magnificent work in searching titles; Carolyn Baldwin and Mary Frances O'Connor for their assistance in the County Recorder's office; the staff of the Clerk's Office in the Madison City Hall; Dennis Babbitt, librarian, and staff members, Jeri McKay, Charlene Peters, and Patricia Selig of the Madison-Jefferson County Public Library; John M. Hollingsworth of Indiana University's Geography Department for the cartography which appears on the book's end sheets; Leigh Darbee and Tim Peterson of the William Henry Smith Library of the Indiana Historical Society; Cindy Faunce, the Indiana Division of the Indiana State Library; and Brooklyn Cull, historian for Historic Madison, Inc.

We are also indebted to editors Kent Calder and Paula Corpuz and assistant Kathy Breen of the Indiana Historical Society's Publications Division for their expert work in connection with the production of the book. Additional thanks go to the many property owners who have graciously supplied information.

Photographs in the book have been supplied over many years by a number of people, including the following: Jack Boucher, official photographer for the National Park Service, the Historic American Buildings Survey (HABS), and the Historic American Engineering Record (HAER); the late Robert Twente, one-time official photographer for Eli Lilly and Company; Dr. Frank Baker, professor emeritus, Hanover College; the W. H. Bass Photo Company and Macklin Thomas, both of Indianapolis; Joe Scheirich, Louisville; and Werner Braun, Ward Poor, and Stephen W. White of Madison. Special mention should be made of the telescopic photographs of architectural details taken by the late Everett German, a part of the collection presented by Mrs. German to Historic Madison, Inc.

Mildred Scott has given invaluable assistance over a period of two years. She has been my observer and my reporter. Following the axiom of Gertrude Stein that "architecture was made for people who go about on their feet," she, with her husband on their daily walks, has studied every building in the town. She has familiarized herself with the terminology of the architectural styles in Madison and has reported back to me with the greatest accuracy those details I may have forgot or overlooked. She has been truly indispensable.

The greatest credit must go to Ann Windle, my wife. She has been my historian, my researcher, my sounding board, and my critic.

When I think of myself and my relation to the book and the many people who have contributed to its making, I see my role as similar to that of ring-master in a circus. The ringmaster appears in a prominent position. He directs the performers by bringing the artists into the ring at the proper moment, and they put on the show. And when the performance is over, the ringmaster takes the bow— for all of them.

John T. Windle

Madison, Indiana
January, 1986

Contents

Buildings

III. Federal

IV. Classic Revival

IX. Mixed Styles

X. Stone Buildings

XI. Railway Station

XII. Firehouses

XIII. Industrial Architecture

Introduction

FORGOTTEN for nearly seventy-five years, Madison during the last half century has increasingly become a mecca for architects and architectural historians. They have come not only to study its architecture but to discover how this small city on the banks of the Ohio River produced some of the most notable architecture in the Old Northwest Territory and how it has miraculously survived. To analyze and record the most stylistically significant extant buildings in Madison is the chief purpose of this book. The geographical, economic, and social factors which contributed to Madison's early architectural development are covered in Robert Taylor's chapter on the city's historial background.

It is interesting to note how Madison got started. Early in the nineteenth century, when the urge to conquer the West was strong in the minds of many people along the eastern seaboard, "The West" meant for the most part nothing farther than Ohio, Kentucky, Indiana, and Illinois. Pioneers came down the Ohio River in large numbers from Pittsburgh and Wheeling in flatboats and on rafts, in canoes and dugouts, to a point where the Michigan Indians had long come to a favored place for crossing the river. To reach this crossing, generations of Indians had worn a deep trail far from the north through the wilderness. This Indian trail, to become known as the Old Michigan Road, served as a ready-made highway for settlers to leave the river and to travel northward in search of fertile farmlands. It was in the vicinity of this juncture of trail and river that settlers, as early as 1806, erected their lean-tos and log cabins and shortly brought into existence the town of Madison. Outfitting the settlers who struck inland at this point became the initial source of the town's income. Later, as they became established on their farms, they drove their livestock through the woods to be put on the paddle wheelers and shipped to New Orleans, the city that consumed nearly everything produced upstream.

Madison grew quickly. Fortunately, among the first wave of settlers following the frontiersmen was a group of men and women of culture and education from the southeastern states, mainly from Virginia, who chose to build their homes in the style which had become popular after the Revolution, the Federal or New Republic. The most distinguished example of this style is the house that was built by the young lawyer Jeremiah Sullivan in 1817–18, barely twelve years after the first log cabins. Madison's growth came at a time when builders had everything in their favor—a great supply of fine wood, skills that were highly developed in all of the building trades, pride in their work, money, and time. It was a period of great interest in architectural styles. Builders' guides and carpenters' handbooks were readily available.

The development of a style is the growth of accumulated taste through a period of time. Any comments on the architectural styles in Madison must make clear that no style leapt into full-fledged being. Instead, any new architectural style evolved from preceding styles. A certain building may have elements of design which are characteristic of one major stylistic tradition and other elements, perhaps, which are characteristic of a preceding period. Also, architectural styles in Madison in the years before and shortly after the Civil War, just as in other midwestern towns, did not always appear consecutively. Different styles were often simultaneously popular. The Classic Revival, including the Greek and Roman, and the Gothic Revival both flourished in Madison in the period approximately from 1830 to 1860. In addition, the time lag of twenty years or longer between the introduction of a stylistic development on the East Coast and its arrival in Indiana meant there was a chance of alteration in the style itself. This interval allowed the possibility of a lack of purity, but at the same time it permitted the development of a distinctive character. To quote Rexford Newcomb, "But, whatever the pattern—classic or Romantic—there is a common quality that indelibly stamps midwestern architecture as different, yet truly American. This quality—the result of a long heritage—is the abiding continuum of that phenomenon which we call 'American architecture.'"[1]

In the following pages comments on specific structures in Madison have been made with these governing principles in mind: the buildings chosen for illustration have been classified, each under a certain style with the design elements characteristic of that style indicated. If the building shows elements of design drawn from other styles, they too are mentioned. Only those elements of style which appear in the buildings in Madison will be described. American architecture of the nineteenth century is rich and varied, and many fine books and articles have been written about it. A broad sampling is listed in the bibliography for those wishing to pursue the subject.

Many other buildings could have been added had space permitted. Nearly all of the nineteenth-century structures on every street contribute to the unique charm of Madison. This architectural richness was recognized nationally when in 1973 the entire downtown, a total of more than 130 city blocks, was placed on the National Register of Historic Places. At that time this area was said to be the largest in the country to be so designated.

This city, with its hills, river, and broad, tree-lined streets, creates an atmosphere of harmony and serenity. It is, however, the diversity of its early architecture, with its overlapping of styles, which gives the town its distinct character, immediately recognizable but difficult to analyze. The late Carl Berg, A.S.L.A., a former consultant to the City Planning Commission, said it briefly and best when he called it "The Madison Look."

1. Rexford Newcomb, *Architecture of the Old Northwest Territory: A Study of Early Architecture in Ohio, Indiana, Illinois, Michigan, Wisconsin and Part of Minnesota* (Chicago: University of Chicago Press, 1950), 161.

To the memory of Wilbur Peat

Historical Background

T HE HISTORIC BUILDINGS of Madison, Indiana, have weathered the years remarkably well. Once the state's leading metropolis, the venerable Ohio River town has managed to keep intact a relatively large number of its nineteenth-century structures. This prime collection of architecture has outlasted that of its riverine neighbors largely because of circumstances peculiar to Madison's development. Madison began its existence in the early 1820s as a port of entry for settlers moving into the interior of Indiana. With the coming of the steamboat in the 1820s the town blossomed into a major river port. The building of the Michigan Road in the 1830s facilitated the passage of travelers and commodities. The construction between 1836 and 1847 of the Madison and Indianapolis Railroad, the state's first, provided Madison with the primary means to tap the trade of its hinterland. The processing of agricultural produce became the foundation of Madison's industrialization. Factory and store, riverboat and train, town and country related in such a way as to propel Madison to the forefront of Indiana's antebellum communities.

The first break in this delicately fabricated web of economic prosperity occurred in the 1850s with the introduction of other railway lines running across Madison's traditional supply region and interacting with Madison's main urban competitors, Cincinnati, Louisville, and Indianapolis. Confronted with a shrinking trading area and a decline in river traffic,

Madison soon lost ground but struggled valiantly to recover its former glory. For several years in the early 1870s a flush economy once more inspired visions of greatness. The bubble burst all too soon, and Madison retreated behind its verdant hills and mostly slumbered. During the following century of little or no growth, the impressive remnant of buildings erected during Madison's palmy days stood fast. We are largely the beneficiaries, therefore, of Madison's economic misfortune.[1]

Madison was established upon a shelf of high ground between the Ohio River and Crooked Creek. A crescent of high bluffs framed the two-mile long tongue of land. In 1808 John Paul, Lewis Davis, and Jonathan Lyons had purchased at the Jeffersonville land office 691.54 acres bordering the Ohio River.[2] To John Paul, a shrewd land speculator, the Madison property possessed several advantages which he and his associates trumpeted in Cincinnati's *Liberty Hall*, January 23, 1811, when they first advertised the sale of lots.

Will be exposed to sale, on Monday the 18th of February, 1811, a great number of lots in the town of Madison, one-half

1. The only scholarly study of antebellum Madison and one that has proved invaluable for this book is Donald T. Zimmer, "Madison, Indiana, 1811–1860: A Study in the Process of City Building" (Ph.D. diss., Indiana University, 1974). See also Zimmer, "The Ohio River: Pathway to Settlement," *Transportation and the Early Nation* (Indianapolis: Indiana Historical Society, 1982), 61–88.

2. Jeffersonville District Tract Book 5: 215 (Archives Division, Indiana State Library, Indianapolis: microfilm A-19).

the purchase money to be paid in one year after the day of sale, and the other half in three years. Madison is established as the county seat in and for the county of Jefferson, Indiana Territory, and is beautifully situated on the bank of the Ohio River, 15 miles below the mouth of Kentucky, and is one of the most healthy and elegant situations on the banks of said river, and near the center of the most fertile country in said territory; its centric situation is occasioned by being situated on the extreme of a very extensive north bend of said river. MADISON will be one of the best stands in the western country, for Mechanics of all descriptions, Merchants, and Gentlemen of Professorial characters, DOCTORS only excepted. Due attendance will be given by Paul, Davis & Lyon.[3]

Easy possession of a county seat's lots, the most direct route to the fertile backcountry, close proximity to the bustling Ohio and Kentucky rivers, a healthy climate, and favorable prospects for commercial greatness — these were the attributes the proprietors wished to emphasize.

The owners of the Madison site could have said much more: that the property lay beside one of the most navigable sections in the Ohio River;[4] that it was convenient to the bustling cities of Louisville, Lexington, and Cincinnati;[5] that the tulip and white oak trees were in abundance for making houses, barns, fencing, farm implements, and boats;[6] and that the climate was particularly suited for growing corn.[7] If completely candid they would have mentioned that Madison's hinterland carried north only about twenty miles; beyond that lay Indian lands. They would have forewarned, if they had known, that the outskirts embodied the least fertile of the region's lands and were the least blessed in mineral resources. They might also have reminded potential buyers that the town site was enveloped in a blanket of timber, right down to the river's edge. Lastly, they would have given notice about the extreme heat of a Madison

summer. To the editor of the Madison *Courier* on a steamy day years later the town did not sit "'like a gem within a coronal of hills verdant to the summit' as a newspaper man at Indianapolis said the other day. To one that's here it doesn't incline to poetry, it appears much liker to a hot potato set down in a circle of embers."[8] But why so hot? The newspaperman theorized that the heaps of rocks, clay, and sand around the town acted like huge mirrors reflecting the sun's rays onto the town.

The proprietors laid out Madison in the familiar grid pattern on the second bank of the Ohio River. The grid generally conformed to the north-south meridian lines and the east-west geographer's or base lines as marked by surveyors, and it did not observe the natural contours of the terrain or of the river. The checkerboard plat encompassed four blocks. Each block contained sixteen squares; each square contained two lots; and each of the 128 numbered lots measured a generous 14,112 square feet. Five straight streets — High, Second, Main Cross, Third, and Back or Fourth — ran east and west. The five intersecting streets were East, Walnut, Main, Mulberry, and West. Main Cross and Main streets, at ninety-nine feet in width, were obviously predetermined to be the primary arteries of trade. The dimension of the other streets was sixty feet. The grid was made to order for the western land speculator and for the eastern and southern migrants likely to inhabit it. It could be laid out anywhere

3. *Liberty Hall* (Cincinnati), 23 January 1811.
4. Zimmer, "Madison, Indiana," 6.
5. In 1810 Louisville had a population of 1,357, Cincinnati 2,540, and Lexington 4,326.
6. Zimmer, "Madison, Indiana," 24–25.
7. Ibid., 32.
8. Madison *Daily Courier*, 28 June 1873.

without regard for topography, or even knowledge of it. The simple, efficient regularity of the plat facilitated lot sales, expedited expansion, lessened litigation over boundaries, and expressed the order and balance familiar to the westward movers.[9]

Critics of the usual town grid in the western country generally found fault with its dreary repetition of evenly spaced lines. In Madison's case there were breaks in the monotony. Not all the streets were the same width, as we have indicated. Nor did they all correspond with the original survey lines of the section. High Street, nearest the river, was laid out without calculating its relation to the true meridian, thus creating irregular lots fronting on the street. In addition, unlike most grids, Madison did not reach to the river. The riverfront was not a part of the town. No streets were to extend south of High Street, although the proprietors stipulated that passage from the south end of every street to the river be opened and unobstructed.[10] Thus, instead of an invariable arrangement of streets and lots extending directly back from the river's edge, Madison's configuration allowed for some relief.

Further deviations from the standard grid accompanied the initial development of the riverfront and the expansion of the town. Streets were eventually graded to the river. A one-hundred foot wide "public highway," Ohio Street, now Vaughn Street, was constructed along the first bank of the river. The eventual platting of the bottomlands produced a string of asymmetric lots because the original plat had disregarded the lineament of the river. Moreover, when the first westside additions were made to the town, in 1815 and 1817, the east-west streets bent northward consistent with the river's outline, and the width of the new roads varied from fifty-six feet to one

hundred and thirty feet.

Clearly, once a successful sale of lots took place, as in Madison, the justification for an efficient and unvaried plat ended, and other considerations came to the fore. A second phase of town building ensued with an emphasis on commercial progress. As additions were made to the original chart of land, Madison began to lengthen out along the riverfront, presenting as broad a face as possible to this major conduit of merchandise. It also began to extend west and north towards the hinterland, towards that abundant food supply presently to be exploited in its processing industries.

Historians typically locate the origins of a town in the formal platting of a tract. Often overlooked, however, is the mid-nineteenth-century generation's inclination, when taking note of its town's roots, to refer to something more tangible, usually a structure of some type. It was commonly known that hundreds of plats were stillborn, mere flights of fancy. The pipe dream and the paper plat characterized much of speculative western town building. Thus in recalling the instant of a community's founding, the idea of laying foundations was taken quite literally to mean a house or a building, however impermanent, because it signified the potential for permanency; it stood for stability.

At the threshold of Madison's existence was a structure, crude and temporary, but nonetheless a piece of design, a work of architecture, broadly understood. John Henry Waggoner and his wife,

9. Carole Refkind, *Main Street. The Face of Urban America* (New York: Harper and Row, 1977), 17.
10. John Paul, "Explanation of the Original Map of Madison" [1824] in untitled record book of street gradings [c.1840] (Clerk's office, City Hall, Madison).

Maria Jane, came to the site of Madison from Pennsylvania in May of 1809 to the foot of what now is Jefferson Street. There they erected a tent-like affair of linen wrapped around four saplings, the whole crowned with the wooden deck of their flatboat. An expedient shelter, obviously, and not even the first in the vicinity for a few families as early as 1806 had settled on the high ridges behind the site. To the next generation, however, the hastily built refuge marked the inception of the town. Whoever wrote Waggoner's obituary in 1841 makes the point that not only did this pioneer, with his flax-walled lodging, erect the first residence in Madison, he also "made the beginning of what is now the city of Madison."[11]

If housing pointed to the moment of a town's birth, it also, in subsequent years, served as a measure of a town's prosperity. For example, in 1850 the editor of the Madison *Weekly Courier* advised his readers that if they wished to judge how far Madison had advanced since its founding they need only look at its building activity, which, he suggested, "furnishes evidences of progress which are better than any language to give a true idea of the growth of Madison."[12] Stacks of building materials on city streets, though annoying to pedestrians, gladdened the heart of every civic booster because they augured progress. "The march of city improvement is still onward. Almost every square is now beautifully decorated with a pile of brick, sand, and mortar," the *Courier* editor declared.[13] Rarely did the local papers pass up an opportunity to register the number of buildings going up in a season, and to boast of their size, costliness, and modern appointments.

The construction business then as now rested to a large extent on the general business climate. For Madison to appreciably develop its stratum of buildings, it had to create a robust economy that would foster jobs and wealth. This meant seeing to it that an expanding hinterland looked upon Madison as the logical market for its produce, that the movement of farm commodities to and from the town and river be practicable, and that the town be organized sufficiently to handle the means of transport and the goods transported.

In 1818 the two-year-old state of Indiana acquired the central third of its domain through a treaty at St. Mary's, Ohio. The New Purchase, as the tract of land was called, afforded Madison access to the rich lands that lay just beyond the town's less fertile surroundings. Before this Eden could be tapped to Madison's benefit, the Delaware Indians had to leave, which they had until 1821 to do, and the land had to be reoccupied and improved enough to yield a marketable surplus crop. In the meantime, Madison served as a distribution point for people and supplies. Settlers coming down river usually bought the bulk of their goods at Pittsburgh or Cincinnati, but persons moving from Kentucky and points south into the New Purchase often sold out at Lexington and resupplied at Madison.

In any case, people and stock had to be housed and fed, as well as provisioned; thus blacksmith shops, general stores, drugstores, dry goods stores, groceries, taverns and stables, as well as residences, dotted the town. Most of these early dwellings were log cabins or log houses, probably of the traditional upland south variety of oak and poplar, half-dove-

11. Madison *Courier*, 29 May 1841.
12. Madison *Weekly Courier*, 23 March 1850
13. Ibid., 1 May 1850.

tailed joints, and set on cornerstones to permit the movement of air. But travelers funneling through the city could also see a number of frame and brick buildings. Carpenters, brickmakers, and stonemasons were on the scene early. In fact some of these craftsmen may have been free blacks. It is reported that C. P. J. Arion before leaving Shelby County, Kentucky, sometime between 1812 and 1817, had his slaves learn brick laying and stone masonry. He then freed them and brought them to Madison.[14] An estimate in 1816 put the numbers of the respective buildings at one hundred cabins, twenty frame houses, and three or four brick houses.[15] Tradition has it that in 1814 John Paul built the first brick structure, a residence, now gone, on the northwest corner of Main and High streets. Other brick structures erected before 1819 included a livery stable and the Farmers and Mechanics' Bank on Main (Jefferson) Street, an octagonal brick courthouse, the Jeremiah Sullivan, the Richard Talbott, and the Robinson-Schofield houses on West Second Street. In 1819 Israel T. Canby built on Main Cross Street probably the town's earliest three-story brick building.[16]

By 1819 Madison had, by local count, 821 inhabitants and 123 dwellings.[17] The federal census the following year gave Madison 984 residents and 133 dwellings. A newspaper in late 1821 reckoned the town had a population of between 1,100 and 1,200 persons.[18] Its status as an incorporated town went into effect April 1, 1824. Madison was growing, but slowly, considering it functioned as the gateway to the most direct route into the New Purchase. A period of nationwide economic decline, extending from 1819 through 1824, along with severe seasons of illness and as yet a relatively unoccupied hinterland, hampered expansion.

The town itself left much to be desired. The riverfront was wilderness. Trees covered the bottomland and overflowed the high bank. Passersby in boats could not have seen Madison for the timber. Town additions continued to be recorded, four between 1822 and 1826. Speculators, however, held on to their properties, gambling on future profits, thus perpetuating empty lots throughout the hamlet. Streets were little more than stump-filled dirt tracks. Ponds, formed by numerous springs, were scattered about the streets further obstructing improvement efforts. Marshland dominated the area of Main Cross and Main (Jefferson) streets, the evolving principal business corner.[19]

What a difference a few years would make. From an obscure and obscured entrepot of the 1820s, Madison by the early 1830s had moved into a paramount position relative to other Indiana cities. It had 1,752 inhabitants in 1830, more than any other community in the state. It was the seat of the wealthiest county, the possessor of one-eighth of all taxable properties in the state in 1835.[20] Madison's transition from a fledgling hamlet to a fledgling urban marketplace was partially a response to increasing pressure

14. See the Arion family file in the Madison-Jefferson County Library.
15. Madison *Weekly Herald*, 26 September 1889.
16. See the Madison *Indiana Republican*, 28 August 1819.
17. Ibid., 23 January 1819.
18. Ibid., 27 September 1821.
19. "Madison Started," undated newspaper clipping, Madison-Jefferson County Library.
20. See undated newspaper clipping in Robert J. Elvin's scrapbook, Madison, 1842–1893 (Indiana Division, Indiana State Library, Indianapolis). The figures used in the newspaper account were taken from the published reports of the state auditor.

from the more than thirty actual and potential rival towns strung along Indiana's southern border.[21] In addition, the demands of a rapidly occupied backwoods pushed Madison to satisfy its neighbors. Most important for the town's future, however, was a series of developments in transportation.

New roads, steamboats, and railroads enabled Madison to take full economic advantage of its setting. The first fifteen miles of the one hundred-foot-wide Michigan Road had been cut and grubbed north of Madison by the fall of 1831.[22] This thruway to Lake Michigan, the cornerstone of the state's aggressive road-building program, expedited Madison's penetration of its tributary area. On another front, steam navigation by the 1830s had become, besides a major industry, the primary means of carrying people and produce west. It almost exclusively accounts for the quickened pace of city growth along the Ohio River. Madison never really challenged Cincinnati or Louisville for commercial supremacy, but the steamboat did greatly enlarge Madison's import and export trade. The "elephant palaces," as some steamboats were aptly called, also exposed Madison as a convenient breakpoint on the Cincinnati-Louisville run. Finally, Madison got into the boat-building business. James Howard, later of the famed Howard yards at Jeffersonville, and Prime Emerson established a boatyard on the eastern periphery of Madison in 1836.[23]

Steamboats brought to Madison an increasing diversity of goods and played an important role in carrying away the articles of farm and factory. To realize fully its business potential, however, Madison required a cheap, swift, land-based carrier. The state granted a charter to the Madison, Indianapolis and Lafayette Railroad Company in 1832, but the firm faltered in financing the operation. In 1835 the legislature authorized a survey for a railroad or a turnpike from Madison to Lafayette. The following year the state's massive internal improvements bill sanctioned a railroad from Madison to Lafayette via Indianapolis.[24] Farmers expressed fears of excessive competition from other farmers along the route of the proposed train. Wagoners thought their occupation doomed. And some citizens warned of oppressive taxation if the state went ahead with its plans.[25] Nevertheless, construction began in late 1836 on Indiana's pioneer railroad.

Although it would take another decade and the railway's completion to Indianapolis before Madison would feel the full economic impact, the mere prospect of rails into the city touched off considerable interest and investment. Indeed, throughout the early to mid-1830s signs appeared indicating a positive economic response to the increasingly rapid interaction of transportation modes. The anticipated construction of some fifty buildings was reported in 1831, a dozen of these to be three stories high.[26] One new establishment, Dearborn and Washer's steam flour mill ("a good merchant mill has long been wanted in this place") rose five levels.[27] Other steam powered mills for processing cotton and castor oil went into operation, as did a foundry and a wagon works. Joseph Reed built a large sawmill, not steam powered, on the east side, the products of which

21. Stephen S. Visher, "The Location of Indiana Towns and Cities," *Indiana Magazine of History* 51(December, 1955): 341.

22. Madison *Indiana Republican*, 15 September 1831.

23. Madison *Republican and Banner*, 1 June 1836, 29 June 1836.

24. Zimmer, "Madison, Indiana," 128–29.

25. See, for instance, Madison *Republican and Banner*, 9 April 1835.

26. Madison *Indiana Republican*, 21 April 1831.

27. Ibid., 19 July 1832.

supplied builders for a decade.[28] The pork packing business, subsequently Madison's premier industry, intensified so much with each passing season that a Wheeling, West Virginia, paper in 1835 declared that "next to Cincinnati, Madison is probably the greatest pork market in the west."[29] Smaller new-born industries produced chairs, hats, and pottery of the "red and black ware" variety.[30] Retail and wholesale houses clustered into several "commercial rows." At least forty dry goods stores and grocery stores dotted the main streets.[31]

The building activity accompanied feverish buying and selling of lots as property values inflated. Huge chunks of land, heretofore withheld pending their future worth, came onto the market. Of particular note was the tendency to dispose of riverside blocks in order to take advantage, as one seller advertised, of the "rapid growth of this place, the increased demand for building lots, and the importance of building and business sites contiguous to the river and the best landing fronting the town."[32] Besides the progress on the riverfront, civic boosters looked to land transactions to help eventually relieve the shortage of housing stock. The lack of living space, the result of a too-rapid influx of settlers and gambling with vacant land, was viewed as a barrier to further expansion. Thus in 1836 when John Burnet offered for sale his unimproved one-sixth interest in the town, the local editor trusted that the sale would "obviate one difficulty now rather stifling the growth of the place—the scarcity of dwelling houses. Many enterprising mechanics and business men are prevented from coming here, at present, because they cannot obtain suitable residences."[33] The topic of inadequate housing, especially for the working class, would crop up again and again in the years to come.

The revolution in transportation and the settlement of the hinterland enabled Madison to start doing more than just subsist and host immigrants. Surplus farm products began to trickle down to the river town. Trade blossomed as growing numbers of customers clamored for more and more goods and as basic food-processing industries yielded an ever-increasing supply of cargo. This harvest of both spreading farmlands and new technologies created wealth which flowed into more land speculation, commerce, manufacturing, and housing.

To help manage that wealth and provide credit for expansion, Madison had the services of a succession of sound banking institutions. The Farmers and Mechanics' Bank, incorporated in 1814 by the territorial legislature, was Indiana's first successful bank. The two-story brick building stood on the east side of Main (Jefferson) Street, above Second Street, throughout its twenty-year chartered history. In 1820 it became a depository of the United States treasury. Its role as a federal depository enhanced its stability, created investor and customer confidence, and consolidated a large supply of funds for loans to farmers and businessmen. When the Farmers and Mechanics' Bank's charter was not renewed in 1835, its functions were taken over by the newly created branch of the State Bank of Indiana. In November, 1834, the semi-private Madison branch opened its doors, and for the next two decades it monopolized banking operations

28. Newspaper clipping, 4 November 1880, in Sophronia S. Lewis Scrapbooks 1865–1892 (Indiana Division, Indiana State Library, Indianapolis).
29. Quoted in the Madison *Republican and Banner*, 16 April 1835.
30. Madison *Indiana Republican*, 18 November 1830.
31. Ibid., 8 September 1831.
32. Ibid., 5 May 1831.
33. Madison *Republican and Banner*, 28 April 1836.

MADISON BRANCH OF THE SECOND STATE
BANK, built in 1834 on the site of the present Madison
Bank and Trust, 215 East Main Street. The building was
torn down in 1954.

Indiana State Library

in the community. From its handsome Greek Revival
edifice on Main Cross (Main) Street, the largely
merchant-owned-and-governed bank distributed a
healthy dividend to its businessmen backers, who in
turn composed the bank's heaviest borrowers.[34]

The nation's inflationary boom of the mid-1830s
fostered a financial panic in 1837, which contributed
to the collapse of Indiana's huge internal improvements program in 1839. The branch bank at Madison was not caught off guard. The local banks had
followed a conservative fiscal policy, rarely exceeding
the levels of circulation specified in their charters.
Their usual ample reserves insured a sound currency
and helped them weather the topsy-turvy world of
nineteenth-century money matters. The panic and
the subsequent depression, however, created such
scarcities in the money supply that even Madison's
branch bank experienced severe reductions. The
cutback in bank operations had its dire effect

throughout the community and added greatly to the
debility the city sustained during the depression.

Not until the mid-1840s did the nation and
Madison begin to climb out of the economic dol-
drums. After years of business failures, lackluster
trade, sheriff sales, and frugality, construction activity
heralded the return of better times. "For five or six
years past," the *Republican Banner* editor observed in
1846, "citizens labored under heavy debt, created
during the apparent prosperity of the years 1836–7
and 8, and consequently but little improvement was
made during that time nor until within a year or two
past. Last year, however, and the present season, a
very large number of large, commodius, and some
very fine buildings have been erected. We under-
stand that there will be erected during the present
year, a much greater number of manufacturing
Establishments and dwellings than have ever been
built in any former year. Without the latter we cannot
increase our present population or build a great
city."[35]

One "very fine" building the editor may have had
in mind was the Lanier mansion. James F. D. Lanier,
president of the Madison branch bank, spent around
$50,000 to have the architect Francis Costigan
design and build his Classic Revival-styled home.
Completed in 1844, its monumental construction
during the economically depressed years of the early
1840s must have aroused mixed feelings within the
community. The house was different. Massive in
form, elaborately detailed, it had a style that was
infrequently observed in the region and that con-
trasted sharply with the far more common and

34. See Zimmer, "Madison, Indiana," 182–89.
35. Madison *Republican and Banner*, 27 May 1846.

simpler Federal style. Madison had extant other Classic Revival buildings, particularly public buildings such as the branch bank and the Second Presbyterian Church, the latter erected in 1835, but nothing in a residential structure to compare with the opulence of Lanier's home. The *Courier* noted the novelty of the building as it was going up: "It is not often that we are presented in the West with any unusual display of architectural magnificence in the construction of private residences. But few have the inclination and fewer the means, to do more than erect a plain and comfortable house, and if these requisites are obtained, they feel not the absence of ornament or embellishment. [The Lanier house] is a departure from this custom."[36]

Despite an improved economic climate, some community leaders detected serious flaws in the pattern of Madison's business. Acknowledging the city's premier position in the state's trade network, these leaders nonetheless recognized that Madison's economy was essentially based on one industry—pork packing—and that it was dependent on one mode of transportation—the railroad—to get the hogs to market. They recognized, several years before the problem would reach a critical stage, that rapidly expanding interior and river cities linked by rival rail lines would make serious inroads into Madison's sphere of commercial exchange.[37]

To offset this probable competition and assure continued progress, Madison needed to make immediate changes in its industrial configuration, its receiving and shipping facilities, and its city services. What frustrated Madisonians most was witnessing money that should be going to finance their city's development filling the coffers of rival towns. For example, much of the wheat channeled to Madison passed through unprocessed to Lawrenceburg, Cincinnati, or Louisville because of a deficiency of local flouring mills. Cloth had to be imported for want of cotton mills to spin and weave textiles. The absence of ironworks meant paying outsiders for heavy machinery, steam engines, railroad ties, and the like. A great many other commodities that could be produced in Madison were being made elsewhere. River freight costs were also draining money from the community because after 1847 it had no shipyards.[38] In short, Madison's creation of a successful railroad worked to its detriment. The investment supported the buildup of other cities because of Madison's lack of a variety of locally finished goods to convey to nearby customers.

If around mid-century Madison set for itself the too-ambitious goal of self-sufficiency, the fact remains that it took giant strides in that direction. Madison's Golden Age was from 1847 to 1854, a period of growth and achievement largely brought on by the full flowering of the railroad and the steamboat. Once again an index of building starts, published in the spring of 1850, furnished a measure of the favorable conditions. A street by street survey turned up a total of 137 construction projects, one-third of these being mercantile lodgings.[39] A year

---

36. Madison *Courier*, 9 December 1843.

37. See for example the letter of "Senex," Madison *Weekly Courier*, 20 March 1847; also, 25 September 1847.

38. Madison *Weekly Courier*, 22 August 1846, 20 March 1847. Boat building in Madison ceased between 1847 and 1852. See Zimmer, "Madison, Indiana," 172–75.

39. Madison *Daily Courier*, 31 May 1850. The Madison *Daily Banner*, in a count of new construction in 1849, recorded 117 brick and stone buildings and 79 frame buildings for a total of 196 buildings (27 October 1849).

later Madison reportedly contained 120 three-story business houses.[40]

Pork processing continued to anchor the local industry. The Madison and Indianapolis Railroad, "annihilating time and space,"[41] increased fivefold the importation of live hogs to the North Madison pens between 1846 and 1851. New packinghouses and

STAR MILLS, 721 West First Street, erected in 1854 by W. W. Page (1810–1882). Originally three stories, this structure stands on the site of a mill erected by Page in 1831. Page owned or had interest in five Madison mills and claimed in the 1830s to have ground the first pure white wheat flour that went to the New Orleans market from Jefferson County.

Frank S. Baker

warehouses sprang up each season until by the early 1850s at least fourteen establishments encircled the city, in addition to the correlative industries that dealt with lard, bristles, skins, and barrels. Among the new warehouses erected was that of George W. Phillips, who in 1851 permitted his building to be used for the only appearance in Indiana of famed songstress Jenny Lind. Thereafter, Phillips's business place was known as the Jenny Lind Pork House.[42] The greatest business was done at David White's Mammoth Cave Pork House, an east end complex of buildings built in 1850. Madison's pork production peaked in 1852–53 when 122,799 hogs were butchered.[43]

Several of the principals involved in the pork trade also engaged in the much-needed making of flour. "Old Enterprise" David White located his five-story Magnolia Mills at Broadway and Ohio streets. William Griffen launched the Palmetto Mills in the lower end of town near the railroad bend in 1847. Charles L. Shrewsbury bought the Palmetto Mills a few years later, enlarged it in 1851, and dominated the regional flour trade thereafter. By 1851 Madison had access to four steam merchant mills, including the new mill of Penniston, Broad and Company across the river at Milton, Kentucky. In 1854 W. W. Page built the Star Mills, part of which building is still extant. With a greater volume of farm produce procurable, entrepreneurs founded breweries and such unusual

40. Madison *Daily Tribune*, 14 July 1851.
41. "Before the railroad era it required two weeks and oftener three to drive hogs from Hendricks County to Madison. A drove of hogs loaded on the cars at Bellville on Thursday was landed at North Madison the same afternoon. This is annihilating time and space" (Ibid., 22 November 1851).
42. Madison *Daily Courier*, 14 November 1850, 28 March 1851; the Madison *Madisonian*, 6 January 1852.
43. Zimmer, "Madison, Indiana," 165. The Madison *Daily Courier* put the 1852–53 figure at 145,203 (31 January 1856).

businesses for the time as a barley and corn malt manufactory.[44]

Horses provided another prominent means of livelihood. Madison had the reputation of being one of the finest horse markets in the region. In the latter 1840s this branch of business increased considerably, paralleling the rise in value of the animals. At least

BROADWAY LIVERY AND FEED STABLES, c. 1912. Still extant at 305–307 Broadway, the building is an example of the many stables constructed in Madison in the nineteenth century.

Indiana State Library

eight livery stables in the city engaged in buying and selling horses in 1851.[45]

Besides treating grain and stock, Madison's capitalists poured money into new foundries, though they never realized the long-coveted rolling mill or nail factory. The Southwestern Car Shop of William Clough and Joseph Farnsworth was a much-heralded addition to Madison's heavy metalwork industries. Begun in 1851, the company produced railroad wheels and cars for lines throughout the Midwest.[46]

River transportation to and from Madison improved considerably during the years of burgeoning commerce. Regular packet service to Cincinnati and to Louisville was instituted in the late 1840s. A new ferry between Madison and Milton began operations in 1851. In the same year, a bridge built over the

Indian Kentuck Creek, east of Madison, promised for the city a rich trade that formerly had gone to Vevay and other points up the Ohio River.[47] Perhaps even more important in facilitating water-bound trade and in boosting Madison's economy was the reestablishment of a shipyard. The Madison Marine Railway, replete with five ways or supports to cradle the hull and a steam sawmill, Madison's first, was constructed in 1851.[48] As steamboat trade increased, the city had to be concerned about its docking facilities. Prior to 1830, when the city established a floating wharf, being unloaded onto mud and river debris often tested the patience of passengers and the durability of merchandise. By 1836, however, four permanent landings had been constructed, all within the limits of the original plat. The next spurt of wharf building, spearheaded by pork packers and millers,

44. David White's Magnolia Mills replaced the one he put in an abandoned mill in the east end near Howard's boatyard and which burned in 1848 (see the Madison *Courier*, 11 September 1847; Madison *Daily Banner*, 11 October 1848). On Shrewsbury's Palmetto Mills see Madison *Daily Courier*, 5 December 1850 and 21 July 1851. On mills generally see the Madison *Republican Banner*, 15 September 1847 and 18 September 1850. For an interesting article on W. W. Page see *The Millstone*, 7(March, 1882), 1, 60. The Indianapolis *Journal* headlined Page as "The Oldest Miller in America." The corn malt factory of William McQuistan was declared locally as the "only manufacturer of this article in the West, with the exception of one house in Ohio" (Madison *Daily Tribune*, 21 October 1851).

45. Madison *Daily Courier*, 11 September 1850, 20 April 1851; Madison *Daily Tribune*, 24 May 1851.

46. Gathered around the Southwestern Car Shop, in the west end of the city, were the homes of the employees, which made the complex a small industrial village. The company went out of business in 1858. See related materials in the Madison *Daily Madisonian*, 14 August 1851; Madison *Daily Courier*, 26 December 1877; Zimmer, "Madison, Indiana," 178–80.

47. Madison *Daily Tribune*, 22 October 1851.

48. Ibid., 20 October 1851, 6 November 1851.

MADISON AND INDIANAPOLIS RAILROAD
CUT. Rock slides proved dangerous in the early days of
the railroad, thus the steep walls shown here were
eventually pared down.

Flora Collection, Indiana State Library

began in the late 1840s. By the middle of the year
1850, when J. F. D. Lanier and John Woodburn
developed their 370-foot landing in the west end,
practically the length of Madison's shoreline was
taken up by wharves.[49]

Changes also took place in land travel. Although
W. P. Stevens began in late 1851 to run his imported
four-horse omnibus daily to Greensburg, getting
traffic to and from the countryside posed difficulties
throughout the period.[50] Roads were primitive and
seasonal; inland waterways bypassed the city; and the
town lay below precipitous bluffs. The railroad, of
course, largely overcame these topographic and
climatic obstacles, steaming year around, barring
heavy snows, accidents, and equipment failures.
When building the Madison and Indianapolis Railroad, workers dynamited the ridges behind the town
to make an incline, the steepest ever engineered in

the United States, on which to move cars between
Madison and North Madison. For years afterwards
the state's newspapers referred to Madison as the
"deep cuttings."

The first permanent railroad depot within Madison's city limits was built in 1843 on the north side of
Ohio Street between West and Mulberry streets. It
was a multistory shed said to be some 150 feet long
by 50 feet wide and accessible on all sides. Increased
business forced the abandonment of this structure
within five years and the erection of a new complex of
terminals about six blocks further west. A pork

MADISON'S FIRST RAILROAD TERMINAL,
shown at far right in this 1846 lithograph. Madison and
Indianapolis Railroad [map] 1846. G. & W. Endicott.
Lith. New York.

Indiana State Library

49. Zimmer, "Madison, Indiana," 47; Madison *Weekly Courier,*
16 May 1850. The city also built a wharf extending from east
of Mulberry Street to connect with the old wharf fronting the
steamboat landing (Madison *Daily Banner,* 9 October 1849).
The city's wharfboat was one hundred feet long, twenty feet
wide, and four feet deep (Ibid., 15 June 1849).
50. Madison *Daily Tribune,* 6 October 1851.

FREIGHT AND PASSENGER STATIONS of the Madison and Indianapolis Railroad, c. 1900. The station's bell now rests on the lawn of the Lanier mansion. The 1937 flood destroyed these buildings.

Flora Collection, Indiana State Library

packer took over the old depot.[51] In 1848 the railroad company purchased for $20,000 a 400-foot square block of ground between Vine and Mill streets. On this site was built a large freight terminal, 346 feet long and 63 feet wide. Draymen had access to the cars from doors that ran the length of the building on both sides. The station's 200-foot sign was thought to be the longest in the state. Attached to the new building was a former porkhouse known as the Flint Building. Railroad authorities converted the Flint Building to waiting rooms and offices for the company, and just north, in 1849, they erected a passenger depot, 270 feet long and 27 feet wide. The bell in the passenger station's cupola tolled departure times, and at its peal a thousand watches were adjusted.[52]

While the railroad was a point of pride for Madisonians, their anxiety about its future value led some persons to attach greater-than-usual worth to the Michigan Road and to other arteries. No doubt the Michigan Road contributed to Madison's welfare; at the least it boosted the wagon-making trade. But despite its preeminence it was a seasonal thoroughfare, and though it was the first major

pathway to penetrate Madison's hinterland, farmers and merchants along the route could and did look northward for markets as well as southward. Still in 1850 it was the most important road leading into Madison, and its straightening and widening was an accomplished fact by the end of the year.[53]

Throughout the nineteenth century numerous schemes were offered up to solve the problem of poor roads. The answer, for many, lay in employing wood in some fashion. The corduroy road of side-by-side logs laid transversely was an early rudimental attempt at a solution.[54] In the mid-1830s Madison's papers brimmed with reports on the feasibility of laying strips of wooden tracks on which wagons could travel, but because the width of wheeled vehicles varied considerably, this quixotic notion quickly faded.[55] The idea of surfacing the entire road with milled boards, however, took hold of the public imagination in the late 1840s and set off a craze for plank road building across the country. Proponents

51. Madison *Courier*, 9 March 1844; Madison *Weekly Courier*, 11 September 1850. It is not clear whether Sering and Penniston or Godman and Sons first occupied the depot as a porkhouse. The latter is referred to as the Old Depot packinghouse in 1851 (Madison *Daily Madisonian*, 20 December 1851; Madison *Daily Courier*, 26 December 1877). The Wymond Cooper Shops eventually utilized the building.

52. See the 1849 and 1850 annual reports of the Madison and Indianapolis Railroad Company. See also the Madison *Weekly Courier*, 31 January 1849; Madison *Daily Tribune*, 15 May 1851; Madison *Daily Courier*, 16 May 1852.

53. Madison *Weekly Courier*, 16 May 1850, 12 June 1850.

54. The water company dug up an old section of corduroy road in 1850 at the intersection of Main and Main Cross streets. According to the account the roadway actually served as a bridge across a pond at the junction (Madison *Weekly Courier*, 22 June 1850). See also the Madison *Weekly Courier*, 17 April 1850, concerning a similar discovery on Second Street.

55. See for example the Madison *Republican and Banner*, 13 November 1834.

argued that plank roads could provide an economical, weather-resistent means of travel, support greater loads of produce, increase the value of timberlands and farms, and save wear and tear on stock and equipment. Madison's city council authorized expenditures of thousands of dollars for shares in four plank roads in Indiana, leading to Hanover and Lexington, Vevay, Napoleon, and Brownstown, and one in Kentucky. No class of improvements in and around the city attracted as much attention, and the completion of the projects led the *Courier* to predict the opening "of a new era in the growth of our city."[56]

The city fathers, most of whom were merchants, were no less concerned with the condition of roadways within municipal boundaries. City streets, as extensions of rural highways for conveying buyers and sellers and their merchandise to proper destinations, seemed to be under constant grading, guttering, and graveling in an unceasing struggle to tame the mud and dust. The need for posting street names and numbering houses was discussed but to no avail. Cluttered sidewalks, stray and dangerous hogs and dogs, great piles of logs for sale daily at major intersections, misparked wagons, and drunken and disorderly citizens multiplied the troubles of Madison's Street Committee.[57]

Market days simply added to the town's congestion, but at least they helped to feed the townsfolk and generate trade for neighborhood merchants. Little wonder then that the merchant, wearing his city official hat, paid particular heed to the erection, regulation, and upkeep of market houses. That a space for a market house had been provided in the original plat indicates its importance. Its stalls brimmed with excess produce from home gardens and nearby small farms. The number of wagons at the curb on market days measured the vitality of local agriculture. The market house also served as an informal and formal gathering place. Town meetings and political rallies often took place there.

Madison had at least five market houses in the nineteenth century. Markets undoubtedly were held on the public square from the earliest days, but the first market *house* about which we have knowledge went up in 1817 or 1818. The *Indiana Republican* gave notice on July 11, 1818, that "those farmers and others who wish to attend regular markets are hereby informed that market will be held every Wednesday and Saturday morning at the market house lately built on the public ground."[58] It may have been this building that an eyewitness later described as consisting of poles laid in the forks of four posts and the whole enclosed with clapboards.[59] The next market house, built in 1825, was more substantially constructed. This one was placed in the middle of Main (Jefferson) Street and extended south from Main Cross Street some sixty feet. Town trustees John Hawes, David Wilson, and John Sering drew up the plans. William Thomas did the brickwork and David Wilson, a skilled furniture maker, did the carpentry. Sering and Wilson supervised the project. The following year the ends and cornice of the building were given three coats of white paint. John Paul was

56. Madison *Weekly Courier*, 5 June 1850. See also the Madison *Daily Madisonian*, 19 September 1851, 16 October 1851, 8 December 1851, and the Madison *Daily Tribune*, 27 November 1851.
57. On the hog and dog nuisance see for example the Madison *Daily Madisonian*, 14 August 1851.
58. Madison *Indiana Republican*, 11 July 1818.
59. "Madison Started," undated newspaper clipping, Madison-Jefferson County Library.

allowed $25 for 5,000 bricks to pave the interior. Added later were a bell, graveled sidewalks, curbs, and guttering. In 1832 the building was lengthened another thirty feet.[60]

As the town grew, the public called for a new market house, one preferably that would not obstruct movement on the street. To this end the city hired Joseph G. Cowden in 1838 to erect a building on Broadway.[61] Meanwhile, the old Main Street building continued in use and underwent extensive renovation in 1843–44. In 1846 county commissioners leased to the city ground on the courthouse square, the Walnut Street side, to put up a fourth market house. The brick-columned structure opened for business November 16, 1850, and a few days later workers dismantled the Main Street facility.[62] By the 1870s the Broadway building had become an eyesore.[63] It was sold at auction for $285 in June, 1874.[64] In late 1875 a new building went up west of Broadway on Main Cross Street between Mill and Plum streets. This building, now the Trolley Barn, was used fully as a market until 1886, at which time its southern section was taken over by the Municipal Electric Light Company. Eventually the electric company occupied the entire facility. In 1896 it was bought by the Madison Light and Railway Company. The Walnut Street market house was sold in 1907 and dismantled to make room for the Middleton park and monument.[65]

In making provision for transporting, warehousing, and processing commodities, Madison had also to bear in mind the comforts of overnight guests. Forward-looking cities of the day ascribed great importance to having a first-class elegant hotel, a feature Madison conspicuously lacked, though eight hotels or inns operated in the 1840s. "I have often

WALNUT STREET MARKET HOUSE, 1850–1907, c. 1900. In the 1850s it was not unusual to find 125 wagons lining the market house and neighboring courthouse.
Flora Collection, Indiana State Library

been made to blush for our city at the remarks made by travelers respecting our public houses," bemoaned a newspaper correspondent in 1846, "and the worst of it was, that I could not contradict them."[66] To end this embarrassment, H. P. Newell had Francis Costigan design the three-story, fifty-room, brick Madison Hotel, which opened with great fanfare in March of 1850. With its opening, the *Daily Tribune* pronounced that Madison had "reversed her reputation of having the state's worst hotels."[67]

67. Madison *Daily Tribune*, 14 July 1851. See also Madison *Weekly Courier*, 11 August 1849, 17 October 1849, 23 March 1850, 3 April 1850, and the Madison *Daily Banner*, 11 December 1848, 20 April 1849, 22 March 1850.

60. Gertrude E. Gibson, "History of Madison Markets, 1825–1906" (William Henry Smith Library, Indiana Historical Society, Indianapolis).

61. Madison *Courier and Constitutional Advocate*, 5 November 1842.

62. Madison *Weekly Courier*, 14 August 1850; Madison *Daily Courier*, 16 November 1850, 21 November 1850.

63. "The old trap of a house still stands on Broadway an obstruction to the thoroughfare and a detraction to the architectural grandeur of the new and imposing buildings recently erected in its vicinity" (Madison *Daily Courier*, 3 February 1874).

64. Ibid., 3 June 1874.

65. Gibson, 28–32.

66. Madison *Republican and Banner*, 10 June 1846.

MADISON HOTEL, 1849–1949, as seen in this 1920s photo as the Jefferson Hotel. This Francis Costigan creation was torn down in 1949.

The Harry Lemen Collection

None of the improvements made in the city around the year 1850 affected more the health and safety of the inhabitants than the establishment of a water system. For years water users depended on rain-filled cisterns, a public spring on Michigan Hill, wells, ponds, creeks, and the river. All of those sources had serious drawbacks. When rain was scarce, cisterns dried up. The public spring demanded a long walk to get to it. Wells had to be sunk to great depths through the city's rock foundation to obtain a good supply of water. Ponds stagnated. Creeks and rivers froze, dried up, flooded, or festered with industrial waste.[68] Periodic outbreaks of cholera and the ever-present threat of fires kept the issue of water before the public. In late 1846 the city contracted with the Madison and Clifton Water Company, Thomas J. Godman, Jr., president, to supply the city with water. Godman built spring-fed reservoirs on his property, where the state hospital is now, and selected Ball and Company's Indestructible Water-Pipe to carry the water. By the end of 1850, the water system was largely in place. In 1852 the city purchased the waterworks and in the ensuing years enlarged them.[69]

Of the many benefits to be derived from a ready

access to water, the expectation of finally being able to protect property from fire was uppermost in the public mind. In the early days the bucket brigades drew water from the river or from wells supervised by a well warden. Water was not always available, and the bucket lines were often tardy, undermanned, or underequipped. An ordinance passed in 1831 required every house to provide for a "good substantial leather fire bucket." Home owners and landlords rushed to buy the bucket only to discover that their new vessels leaked. The manufacturer of the buckets, G. W. Bantz, had to recall them and correct the fault at no charge to the customer.[70]

Another fire-related ordinance, effective in 1830, followed the example of larger cities and excluded the erection within the city limits—Main to West, High to Third—of frame or log buildings "to be occupied for the purpose of either dwelling houses, stores, groceries, stables or workshops."[71] This measure, like so many other fire deterrent regulations, carried implications beyond the intent of the law. The immediate effect of limiting building materials to brick or stone may have been a slowdown of construction within the restricted area due to the higher cost of masonry. Those persons wanting the more economical wooden house possibly went ahead with

68. Madison experienced two major floods prior to 1850. In 1832 the flooding of the Ohio River destroyed some half-dozen houses that by that time had located on the river bottom. In 1846 Crooked Creek overflowed killing eleven persons and sweeping away numerous dwellings and factories (Madison *Indiana Republican*, 16 February 1832; Madison *Weekly Courier*, 5 September 1846; Madison *Republican and Banner*, 9 September 1846).

69. Madison *Weekly Courier*, 13 February 1850, 23 May 1850; Madison *Daily Madisonian*, 5 March 1852.

70. Madison *Indiana Republican*, 21 March 1831, 1 September 1831.

71. Ibid., 28 October 1830.

their plans outside the corporate boundaries. If so, the edict contributed to the town's expansion. In 1844 the council extended the law's coverage to encompass the blocks between West and Broadway streets with the added proviso that anyone could put up "wood sheds, privies, and salt sheds."[72]

Without better means of battling fires and without trained and organized firemen and sufficient equipment, ordinances had little worth. In 1831 a Volunteer Fire Fighters Club formed, and a year later the city purchased a small hand pumper. How inadequate were these steps can be surmised from an 1839 editorial in which the writer reminded readers that Madison had no efficient engines, hooks, or ladders, and no organized company. "We have one or two engines, or at least things designated by that name, without the necessary apparatus."[73] The next year the editor wondered how many houses had been supplied with fire buckets![74] In the 1840s the rapid growth of the city and some devastating fires, such as the 1845 blaze which destroyed the First Presbyterian Church and several dozen other downtown buildings, gave new urgency to the problem of fire control. The city chartered three volunteer fire companies in the decade, passed still more fire codes, and allowed for the purchase of larger hand pumpers. By 1851 the first of twenty-five fire plugs was connected to the new water lines. Not until 1860 would Madison have the services of a steam pumper, and not until 1869 would it have a horse-drawn steamer.[75]

Madison built the state's first gasworks. The Madison Gas-Light Company, incorporated January 16, 1850, was granted the right-of-way through the city streets and alleys for twenty years and directed to lay 7,000 feet of pipe before February 1, 1853. The brick gasworks was placed on a 40-square-yard lot

on the corner of Walnut and Ohio streets.[76] The process of making artificial gas involved baking or distilling coal in airtight retorts or ovens and piping off the gas. Water was needed both as a safety precaution and to help purify the gas. A masonry cistern, 50 feet wide and 16 feet deep, held the water. The gasometer for holding and measuring the gas was nearly the same dimensions. In August, 1851, workers placed on top of the building a wrought-iron framework produced at the Neal Iron Foundry and Machine Shop. In describing this phase of the construction the *Courier* reporter made the timely observation that before long iron would take the place of wood in building houses in America as well as in England.[77] That same month the company began laying iron pipe throughout the city. Two months later the City Council ordered 80 lamp posts from the Madison Foundry, and two days before Christmas, 1851, a dinner was held celebrating the dawn of the city's illumination by gas.[78]

72. Madison *Republican and Banner*, 25 September 1844.

73. Madison *Weekly Courier*, 21 December 1839.

74. Ibid., 6 February 1840.

75. On the Presbyterian Church fire see the Madison *Republican and Banner*, 26 March 1845; Madison *Courier*, 22 March 1845. On Madison's firefighting development see Kim Kring, "History of Firehouses in Madison," *The Way It Was: Glimpses into the Past of Madison and Jefferson County* (Madison, Ind.: Madison Consolidated School Corp., 1975), 45-48, and *Madison's 175th Anniversary Commemorative Book* (Madison, Ind.: Commemorative Book Committee, 1984), 36.

76. Madison *Daily Courier*, 28 January, 25 March 1851. A Mr. Lockwood, who, according to the newspapers, was involved in constructing gas works in Indianapolis, Chillicothe, and Steubenville, Ohio, supervised the Madison project (ibid., 12 May 1851).

77. Ibid., 21 July 1851.

78. Madison *Daily Madisonian*, 3 October 1851; Madison *Daily Courier*, 3 December 1851.

The geographic, economic, and populational growth of Madison contributed to changes in its spatial arrangements. Concentrations of commercial, industrial, and residential structures began to develop. America's small town classic Main Street emerged as retailers and wholesalers converged on Main Cross Street. In 1850 much of the commercial activity was localized in a one-block area between West and Mulberry streets, with the rest of the stores and offices stretching east one block to the courthouse square, and west some four blocks to just past Broadway Street. Other businesses ran south along West and Mulberry to the river. Within these areas

VIEW OF THE CITY OF MADISON, INDIANA, from *Gleason's Pictorial Drawing Room Companion*, July 8, 1854.

Indiana Historical Society

were a few observable subgroupings. Dry goods merchants dominated the primary business block. Commission and forwarding houses occupied the riverfront at the foot of West and Mulberry streets. Hotels were on Mulberry and Main streets. Even then numbers of taverns had situated on Mulberry Street, which in subsequent decades would be designated Whiskey Chute.[79]

As a rule, Madison's industries located on the outskirts near water, railroad tracks, and turnpikes. Between the factories and the rather narrow and crowded bands of downtown mercantile houses stood residential neighborhoods already being defined by wealth, race, or nationality. For example, the social and economic elite gravitated to the city's near west side between First and Third streets. The Irish, who had come to Madison to work on the railroad, tended to live in the far western section alongside the railroad tracks. The Germans, brewmasters and skilled workmen, generally preferred the east side of town, east of the courthouse and north on Walnut Street. Madison's blacks, at this time roughly five percent of the population, congregated in a northeast pocket surrounded by German families and factories.[80]

Madison's urbanization also affected the architectural anatomy. A new jail and a courthouse were completed in 1850 and 1855, respectively. The courthouse's bell tower joined the spire of Christ Episcopal Church as a landmark on the city's skyline.[81] In fact the entire courthouse square underwent considerable change. The "Lawyers' Block," a line of offices that stood in front of the jail, was removed exposing the new jail to streetside view.[82] Old frame houses were cleared from the Main Street

79. The arrangement of businesses outlined here was obtained by plotting on a map an extensive, but by no means complete, listing of firms in the Madison *Daily Tribune*, 8 April 1851. The reference to "Whiskey Chute" is found in the context of remarks by publisher M. E. Garber in the Madison *Courier*, 16 May 1952.
80. See Zimmer, "Madison, Indiana," 54–72.
81. See Madison *Daily Courier*, 12 September 1855, 17 September 1855, 8 December 1855, 20 December 1855. The Madison *Daily Banner* (20 December 1848) observed that the Christ Church spire was the only one in Madison at that time.
82. Madison *Weekly Courier*, 22 May 1850.

edge of the yard between the alley and Main Cross Street. An iron fence, 420 feet long, was installed on the grounds bordering Main and Main Cross streets, while a stone-capped brick wall guarded the alley on the south side.[83] For the first time the square became truly a public area with only the jail, the courthouse, and the Walnut Street market house occupying the premises.

The Classic idiom as used in the courthouse remained the popular choice for public buildings and residences. The moderately embellished box-like structure seemed to satisfy a need for economy and proportion. Unlike New Albany, where a writer in the *Bulletin* complained that his city "looks as though it had been pitched together, or the houses as though they had dropped from a seive," Madison maintained an air of regularity in its buildings.[84] At the same time, however, the structural make up of the city grew more complex. The shanties of Irish Hollow, the infinite number of small workshops, and the diverse shapes and sizes of factories, warehouses, and depots added texture to the city's fabric.

Also at this time Madison was introduced to the anti-Classic and more dynamic Gothic Revival style of architecture. The scroll-sawed wooden barge boards that hide projecting roof timbers on the gabled facades of many small houses or cottages in Madison's neighborhoods attest to the popularity of folk Gothic in the Civil War era. Even the Southwestern Car Shop was in 1855 designing railroad passenger cars in the "Gothic style."[85] As early as the 1850s then, with the appearance of Gothic and some Italianate forms, Madison's architectural landscape showed signs of variegation.

Of course, design considerations were inconsequential if land was unavailable on which to build, and

building lots were then at a premium. Still, John Woodburn, for instance, easily disposed of seventy-eight unimproved parcels in the spring of 1850.[86] To find more space for houses and factories within the corporate limits, some persons looked to the hillside bordering on Michigan Road and Sixth Street. The appeal here was the relatively cheap land and the existence as a building material of good quality blue limestone. Several quarries opened on the slope in the early 1850s.[87] For others, the straightening of Crooked Creek offered the greatest potential for stretching Madison's real estate. The correctly named stream absorbed a lot of land area by its twistings and turnings. Uncurling the serpentine creek became a hotly agitated issue, and beginning in 1852, the city worked to rectify what nature intended.[88]

The timing of the appearance of successive architectural styles in Madison rested on a combination of circumstances that included the origins of settlers, the pace of settlement, the skills of carpenters and builders, contacts with trained architects, an informed public, and internal and external town rivalries. Economic conditions also played an important role in the progression of innovative building designs. As Wayne Andrews notes, "The most vital American architecture of any given time will usually be located in those communities where the most new money was being made and enjoyed."[89] By the same token, a faltering economy could disincline persons to take an

83. Ibid., 15 March 1855, 17 September 1855.
84. Quoted in the Madison *Daily Tribune*, 31 May 1851.
85. Madison *Daily Courier*, 12 September 1855.
86. Madison *Weekly Courier*, 30 May 1850.
87. Madison *Daily Tribune*, 22 April 1851, 16 May 1851.
88. Madison *Daily Madisonian*, 3 October 1851, 25 March 1852.
89. Wayne Andrews, *Architecture, Ambition, and Americans: A Social History of American Architecture*, rev. ed. (New York: Free Press, 1978), xxiii.

interest in architecture. This is essentially what happened after 1853 in Madison with the withering of the city's prosperity. Not until the early 1870s could Madisonians once again indulge to any extent in novel building ideas.

Madison's troubles of the 1850s came about largely because competitive railroads choked off the city's hinterland trade at the same time that the general growth of railroads curtailed the formerly heavy river commerce. As early as the spring of 1846 Louisville papers predicted that a railroad from that place to Columbus, Indiana, would draw off two-thirds of Madison's trade.[90] The following year Madison's newspapers outlined five pending railroad projects to transverse the rural section north of the city.[91] The Gate City, as Madison preferred to advertise itself, fought against these intrusions by pushing through its own line and arranging for the building or use of feeder lines. But in 1853–54 Indianapolis trains secured a rail link to Cincinnati and to the eastern seaboard, and the Ohio and Mississippi Railroad connected Cincinnati with Louisville via the Jeffersonville line at Seymour. As a result of these and other railroad developments on both sides of the river, Madison's trading area shrank to little more than Jefferson County.

Madison's difficulties were compounded by what the public perceived as the scandalous administration of the Madison and Indianapolis Railroad Company. For one thing much of the road's stock had been sold to outsiders, mostly New Yorkers, who it was thought were insensible to the vital connection between the M & I and the fate of Madison's economy.[92] Second, the media had a heyday with the so-called Madison Railroad War, a war of words between Michael G. Bright, a state legislator from Madison,

and John Brough, the president of the M & I. Rumors of a collusion to have the M & I purchase the unsuccessful Edinburg and Shelbyville Railroad, owned by Bright, in exchange for legislative favors led to a lively interchange and mutual recriminations between the two parties. The incident degenerated into a burlesque when a duel was intimated and the press gleefully contemplated the fairness of such a contest between Bright and the 400-pound Brough. This embarrassment was succeeded by a more serious episode. With good intention, Brough started work in 1852 on a new track from Madison that would bypass the troublesome incline. The line snaked northwesterly through the rugged terrain of present Clifty Falls Park. After partially completing the grade, evidence of which can still be seen, the project was abandoned in 1855, having up to that point cost over $3,000,000.[93] An angry citizenry linked this waste of money with the general failure of Madison's moneyed men to promote manufactures and to lower rates on unimproved lots, thus providing jobs and affordable housing for workers. As a consequence, it was reported, the town's mechanics, including "brickmakers, layers, and house carpenters" sought work elsewhere.[94]

The speculative mania, which furnished the wherewithall for the growth of competitive railroads, was a national phenomenon affecting all walks of life. If Madison's skilled laborers migrated in droves because of overconcentration on railroad building, they, along with the small and great merchant, were additionally injured when the cash flow dried up and

90. Madison *Weekly Courier*, 14 March 1846.
91. Madison *Courier*, 25 September 1847.
92. See Madison *Daily Courier*, 1 May 1857.
93. See the John Brough and Michael G. Bright clipping files in the Madison-Jefferson County Library.
94. Madison *Daily Courier*, 7 July 1856.

railroad construction slowed. For years individuals, businesses, and banks poured funds into East Coast money markets for use in western railroad and land speculation. As currency became scarce because of the removal of European investments and uncertainty of continued railroad expansion and profit, creditors called in their loans. This action put an unbearable squeeze on thousands of debtors who could not get their hands on ready cash. The deterioration of this shaky financial structure precipitated a brief panic in 1851 and a more severe one in 1857. In the intervening years scores of Madison's businessmen, as in other communities, closed their doors or defaulted on loans, the most sensational case of bankruptcy being that of David White, the city's leading pork packer.[95]

The pork trade, in fact, suffered a conspicuous reversal. The number of hogs slaughtered fell by one-half between the record high season of 1852–53 and that of 1855–56, thereafter continuing the downward trend.[96] Madison's porkhouses simply could not contend with the many new entrants in the business in Indiana and elsewhere that had grown up with an expanding railroad system. More specifically Madison's shippers could not cope with the prohibitive freight rates intentionally imposed on them by rival rail companies for the use of their lateral lines to move goods to and from Madison.[97] Madison's pork kings also faced the 1854–55 season with enormous inventories of unmarketable hog products and delays in opening the trade because of price disagreements between packers and feeders.[98] Moreover, the weather did not cooperate. A terrible drought in the summer of 1854 followed by an extremely cold winter allowed only intermittent river transportation. The dry summer also ruined crops so that another year had to transpire before the farmer and merchant

could hope to recover enough cash, in an already tight cash market, to conduct business as usual. But prospects proved bleak as the next two winters caused suspensions of navigation on the Ohio River for sixty-three and forty-nine days respectively, the most protracted freeze ups of the Ohio between 1846 and 1878.[99]

For these and other reasons, such as the removal of J. F. D. Lanier to New York (c. 1850) and disastrous fire losses at Magnolia Mills (1854), Madison Marine Railway (1856), and Palmetto Mills (1858), Madison experienced a drain of skills and riches, a diminished economy, and, not least, an image problem. An Evansville paper in late 1853 already referred to Madison as "the sinking ship."[100] The following year, as Madison prepared to host the state fair, the *Courier* editor urged manufacturers to display their products to show all attending that Madison was not a "finished" city, but a "finishing" city.[101] True, Madison's remaining industries yet produced a broad sampling of articles including starch, boilers, washboards, railroad cars, saddletrees, plows, flour, beer, lard oil, sash and doors, and bells. The Madison Board of Trade, founded in

95. Zimmer, "Madison, Indiana," 213. The bankruptcy of David White was considered "one of the hardest blows to the business of the city. Her shipyards, manufacturers, and general business will feel the blow adversely for some time" (Madison *Daily Courier*, 28 March 1856). See also ibid., 14 May 1856, on the dissolution of White's residential properties.

96. Ibid., 31 January 1856.

97. Ibid., 2 May 1853.

98. Ibid., 8 November 1854, 23 November 1854.

99. Ibid., 5 December 1854, 7 March 1855, 27 September 1855, 14 January 1857, and undated clipping entitled "Suspension of Navigation" in Elvin scrapbook.

100. Madison *Daily Courier*, 20 December 1853.

101. Ibid., 29 September 1854.

1857, reported 138 establishments engaged in "mechanical and manufacturing pursuits" with output valued at $2.7 million.[102] Still, industrial statistics for Jefferson County in the decade of the fifties reflect Madison's hardship. Whereas the county led the state in 1850 in most manufacturing categories, by 1860 it had slipped to third, even sixth place in some classifications. Meanwhile Madison's resident count increased by only 2 percent in the decade, a far cry from the doubling of population in previous decades. Now, on the eve of the Civil War, Indianapolis not Madison was clearly Indiana's primary city.[103]

Madison in the Civil War exhibited the full register of excitement, agitation, and affliction that accompanied the prosecution of this intestine struggle. So near the South, Madison's sympathies were divided until the firing on Fort Sumter and Kentucky's declaration of neutrality. Then public opinion swung conclusively to the North. Apart from organizing military companies, manufacturing supplies, caring for refugees and the wounded, burying hometown casualties, sheltering fugitive slaves, parading, and preparing for rumored rebel raids, daily life centered on making a living under abnormal circumstances.

Notwithstanding the universal problems of high prices, depreciating currency, scarce labor, and interrupted trade with the South, Madison's economy improved considerably over that of the previous decade. Leading the way were Madison's two shipyards, the Madison Marine Railway, rebuilt after the fire in 1856, and the Dry Dock Company, established in the early 1860s. Foundries flourished by supplying the engines for the steamboats. Crawford and Davidson's Indiana Foundry, for example, employed sixty hands, the largest number of workers, from notice given, of any Madison foundry up to that time.[104]

Though building for the southern trade stopped during the war, the need for new or repaired watercraft to provision or transport the army revitalized shipyards and ironworks all along the Ohio River. Boat painters shared in the general prosperity. Ship carpenters, who in August, 1861, were described as having been out of work for a long time, many compelled to leave the city, found their services in great demand by 1863. At one point the shipyards had to recruit fifty carpenters from outside Madison.[105] Other jobless carpenters in 1861 subsequently found work erecting new business houses. In August of 1863 the *Courier* reported that no less than thirteen new houses were being put up on Main Cross Street alone.[106] Some of the new commercial structures had iron fronts, the first use in Madison of what a few years later became the standard material for modernizing Main Street businesses. Samuel J. Smith's clothing store, erected in 1859 and equipped with an iron facade designed and fashioned by Crawford and Davidson's foundry, was probably Madison's earliest iron front.[107]

Carpenters also found work, at two dollars a day, on the United States General Hospital, erected in 1863 on the old fairgrounds west of the city in the vicinity of the present Madison Country Club. On about thirty acres surrounding a grove of trees was

102. Madison *Daily Evening Courier*, 4 March 1857.
103. In 1850 Madison vied with Indianapolis and New Albany for population supremacy, each having slightly over 8,000 residents. By 1860 Madison had been surpassed by Evansville, Fort Wayne, Lafayette, Terre Haute, New Albany, and Indianapolis. Indianapolis led all cities with a population of 18,611.
104. Madison *Daily Courier*, 18 April 1863.
105. Ibid., 1 May 1863.
106. Ibid., 25 August 1863.
107. Ibid., 13 May 1859.

built one of the North's largest military hospitals. Some 150 carpenters and other craftsmen fashioned 65 one-story wards, each 112 feet long by 25 feet wide. Other structures included dining rooms, a riverside laundry, a stable, a bakery, an ice house, and various offices. The whitewashed buildings, bordering on graded and graveled streets and walks, seemed to one observer "like a neatly laid out New England village of tastefully white cottages."[108] The complex was enclosed by a board fence, eight feet high. Over 8,000 patients were treated in the hospital in its two-year history. In 1864 another group of twelve buildings went up just east of the hospital. The barracks and offices housed the Veteran Reserve Corps, which was made up of war casualties unable to perform further on the battlefields yet capable of doing alternate service. In Madison the veterans guarded the hospital.[109]

Even before the war terminated, suggestions surfaced regarding the eventual use of the hospital and barracks. One plan called for making them a permanent home for disabled soldiers and their families, while another advised converting them to industrial use, a cotton mill perhaps.[110] What actually happened was that after the hospital closed in September, 1865, a reported 143 buildings were auctioned off. Some remained on the grounds, fixed up as rental properties. The rest were torn down or moved to other lots.[111] In 1866 the papers noted that on the former hospital grounds a small community was evolving, embracing besides the homes of "many highly respectable families, . . . the shipyard, a sash factory, a daguerrean gallery, astrologer, retired newspaper editor, and a preacher."[112] But in 1869 hospital buildings were still being dismantled and sold for lumber or relocated.[113] Five years later the papers noted that only one building remained to mark the

place of the facilities.[114] Today it is believed that many of the shotgun-type cottages in and around the city, particularly in the west end, are in fact wards or barracks from the Civil War institutions.

The war-related surge of commerce rolled on into the postwar decade. Some concern was initially expressed that the resolution of the conflict would put an end to some lucrative enterprises. Certainly job holders and suppliers connected with the hospital faced readjustments, as did the boarding houses and hotels that overflowed with military personnel and the few businesses making war materials. On the other hand, everyone anticipated a new round of profit taking when the servicemen returned. Many figured that the shipyards would recover because of the large numbers of boats destroyed, the scrapping of old boats that had been temporarily fixed up for duty, and the reopening of legitimate channels of trade with the South.[115]

In point of fact, Madison's traditional industrial base remained relatively unchanged throughout the sixties. Madison's top ten industries in 1869 in terms of taxable wealth were pork and lard, flour, starch,

108. Ibid., 18 August 1863. Madison's first military hospital was established in the spring of 1862 on West Street. It existed for only a few months before being declared unfit as a hospital for want of ventilation. Shrewsbury and Price's large pork house was earmarked for hospital use if the need arose (see ibid., 31 May 1862). On the building of the United States General Hospital see ibid., 28 February 1863, 4 March 1863, 14 March 1863, 19 March 1863, 27 March 1863, 28 March 1863, 6 April 1863, 9 May 1863, 14 May 1863, 23 May 1863, 18 July 1863, 12 August 1863.
109. Ibid., 21 March 1864.
110. Ibid., 2 May 1865.
111. Ibid., 8 September 1865, 15 September 1865, 25 September 1865, 29 September 1865.
112. Ibid., 30 April 1866.
113. Ibid., 2 March 1869.
114. Ibid., 3 October 1874.
115. Ibid., 9 February 1865, 26 May 1865.

barrels, boats, clothing, furniture, leather, woolen goods, and engines, in that order.[116] In addition, the count of breweries, brickyards, and saddletree factories increased to five each. Supporting these industries was an influx of smaller companies producing such things as brushes, hollowware, hoop skirts, vinegar, syrup, school desks, coffins, and soda fountains. There was some truth to the *Courier's* statement in 1869 that "the large jobbing trade and the rush of strangers of twenty years ago we have not now. Instead we have increased manufactures in all departments. The progress of Madison has been slow compared to Indianapolis, but evidently there has been progress."[117]

The rush of trade between 1863 and the mid-1870s spurred city fathers to undertake and encourage improvements. The council itself increased by three representatives, from nine to twelve, as a result of redistricting the city from nine to six wards with two councilmen instead of one from each ward.[118] Elections after 1867 were held every two years instead of annually. Officials tackled the unremitting tasks of opening new streets and alleys, bridging gutters, constructing culverts and sewers, and repairing road surfaces and sidewalks. They also grappled with the long-discussed issues of changing street names, putting up street signs, and numbering buildings and houses. Many proposals for supplanting the then current system of street names were entertained, ranging from a simple numbering scheme to changing West Street to Central Avenue and naming the streets east of it after trees and those west after presidents starting with Washington. Actually only the change of Cherry Lane to Central Avenue took place in this period. The idea of painting street names on every lamp post was never taken seriously. The

council in 1866 did pass a house numbering plan, with West Street as the divider and every twenty-five feet of ground constituting a number.[119] Except in the downtown business district the actual affixing of numerals to respective structures took years to implement.

While streamlining the city's administration and facilitating the finding of streets or buildings, officials failed in their attempt to erect a new city hall, the construction of which would have halted the expense of renting offices. The proposed two-story brick hall, designed by John R. Temperly, provided as well for market and opera houses. The $29,000 structure would have been situated on the southwest corner of Walnut and Main Cross streets, but bad timing killed the project. Put forward as citizens reeled under the effects of the 1873 panic, a public referendum defeated the measure.[120] In palmier days the council successfully financed a new high school and a waterworks. A spring-fed reservoir, the largest of the three city-owned reservoirs, was built on Telegraph Hill, northeast of the city, in 1868.[121] The water source soon proved inadequate, and in 1870–71 a new waterworks was constructed utilizing steam pumps to draw river water to the big reservoir.

The prosperity experienced prior to the 1873 panic brought forth fresh efforts to beautify the city. Each spring the press urged residents to plant shade trees and shrubs in their yards and paint their houses. The city and county were asked to set out saplings

116. Ibid., 15 December 1869.
117. Madison *Daily Evening Courier*, 30 December 1869.
118. Madison *Daily Courier*, 9 February 1867, 8 March 1867.
119. Ibid., 6 August 1866. See also ibid., 9 February 1866, 13 July 1866.
120. Ibid., 31 December 1873, 6 March 1874, 6 May 1874.
121. Ibid., 29 October 1868, 10 August 1870.

around public buildings. The dozen private fountains and the one public fountain, put up in 1872 in the courthouse square, were often taken as evidence of the town's attractiveness.[122] Old habits and industrialization, however, continued to threaten Madison's natural environment and the health of its people. The problem of filth on walkways, in streets, and behind buildings remained unsolved despite sewer construction and cleanup efforts by the Committee on Garbage (and by the insatiable hogs, which still roamed the town at will).[123] The corralling of the swine after 1873 in a new Hog Pound at High and Main streets helped arrest that nuisance but left the trash question unresolved.[124] Nor had much been done about Crooked Creek. For years the stream had been a receptacle for all types of waste, from animal carcasses to factory pollutants. This health hazard was dealt with in three unsatisfactory ways: passing unenforceable ordinances against dumping, advocating removing the water and filling the ditch with dirt, and praying for rain and a slight flood to wash out the porkhouses and clear the creek of refuse. In the postwar years a new threat to the environment surfaced, or at least was finally recognized. Coal soot and dense smoke from factory chimneys was making the city dirtier year by year. The *Courier* advocated that all establishments consuming over five bushels of bituminous coal daily be forced to put a device called a smoke consumer on their smokestacks.[125] Clearly, Madisonians were becoming more aware of the negative side of industrial progress.

To defray the costs of city services officials relied on taxes and fees which never seemed sufficient for municipal needs. Occasionally a lone voice would speak out for annexing surrounding neighborhoods in order to broaden the tax base. Madison was virtually surrounded by small villages and major manufacturers. Abutting the city to the west and east were West Madison and Fulton respectively. North of Fifth and Walnut streets a community called Georgetown had grown up around Johnson and Clements's starch factory and several breweries. On the hilltop were Fairmount and North Madison. Not until late in the century, however, did the process of absorbing these areas begin.

New forms of recreation emerged in the postwar years, and Madison was not far behind larger cities in adopting them. Consider the velocipede, the forerunner of our chain-driven bicycle. Bonner and Beach, carriage manufacturers, put out the first Madison-built velocipede in February, 1869, from a design of A. M. Connett, an architect. What marred its introduction was the inability of anyone to ride the "steed" before it "lay down." With practice Madison's young men got the better of the "machine," and by March a Velocipede Club had formed and was giving exhibitions of riding skills on the third floor of Trow and Stapp's warehouse and in Columbian Hall. Except for monopolizing the sidewalks, injuring a few riders, and posing a threat to livery stables, the velocipede, or "swift walker," gained the approval of young and old.[126]

Indoor ice skating also came into vogue in the latter 1860s. John Todd opened his frame rink at Poplar and Ohio streets the day before Christmas, 1868. The rink was the state's second, after Indian-

---

122. Ibid., 1 July 1872, 17 June 1874.

123. Ibid., 20 February 1874.

124. Madison *Weekly Citizen*, 25 October 1873.

125. Madison *Daily Courier*, 10 August 1874.

126. Ibid., 4 February 1869, 9 February 1869, 11 February 1869, 18 February 1869. W. S. "Billy" Longacre invented and manufactured a velocipede in March, 1869, referred to in the press as a "tricycle" (ibid., 19 March 1869, 25 March 1869).

apolis's, and claimed to be its largest. The structure was about the size of half a football field and, besides the rink itself, included galleries, dressing rooms, skate repairers room, and ice cream saloon. Fire plugs flooded the rink, and fifty gas burners illuminated it. Its life as an ice skating rink lasted only a few months because of difficulties keeping the water frozen. Todd then laid in a wood floor for parlor (roller) skating and velocipede riding. After the owner died in 1874 Pattie, Smith and Company, lumber merchants and builders, bought the building, tore it down, and constructed an office on the site.[127]

Another favorite resort was the west end's Beech Grove Driving Park. Several years before the development of the park in the early 1870s the public learned that some of the trees in the grove were being cut down, probably to be used for fuel as other timber stands dwindled. At the time the grove, owned by Jesse Whitehead, was considered the only convenient place for outdoor gatherings, although there was talk of converting the old cemetery on Third Street to a park, which eventually did occur.[128] Not only the grove's trees but those along the river road, a favorite driving route, were being leveled. The subsequent public outcry no doubt influenced the improvements at the grove, for indeed it was a cherished spot, the centerpiece of the 1854 state fair and the Civil War hospital. In the summer of 1875 the Beech Grove Trotting Park Association was formed. Its stockholders purchased the Whitehead and Hunter properties encompassing the grove and the Hunter mansion. The Association talked the county fair board into moving its annual agricultural fair from North Madison to the new park. Several structures, including the amphitheater, were removed to the new grounds. A half-mile race track was erected along

THE BEECH GROVE DRIVING PARK as it appeared on an early twentieth-century postcard.

with stables and a baseball diamond in the track's infield. A high board fence girdled the park's forty-two acres. That fall the Jefferson County Agricultural Fair held its annual exhibition of farm products and livestock at Beech Grove, and the facilities remained popular for many years afterwards.[129]

The establishment of a street railway in 1874 afforded an advanced means of travel through the city. Mule-drawn omnibuses had been the standard conveyance for several years before the incorporation of the Madison Street Railway Company. The new cars, a "commodious model of the Pullman sleeper on a small scale," measured about nine feet long inside with a carrying capacity of eighteen passengers. Four-horse teams initially pulled the cars along Main Cross Street on a track running from Walnut Street to the railroad bridge, a distance of almost two miles.

127. Ibid., 23 October 1868, 13 November 1868, 2 December 1868, 14 December 1868, 22 December 1868, 24 December 1868, 25 February 1869, 23 April 1869; Madison *Weekly Citizen*, 17 January 1874, 28 March 1874.
128. Madison *Daily Courier*, 23 March 1874, 27 April 1874.
129. Ibid., 2 December 1875; Madison *Daily Evening Star*, 23 June 1877.

The line soon was extended north on Walnut Street and east along Second Street to Ferry Street.[130]

Much has been written about the effect of the streetcar on the character of late-nineteenth-century American cities, not all of which holds true for Madison.[131] Here, the streetcar did not make possible a geographically larger city, because Madison proper and its satellite villages below the hills had nowhere to expand. The fixing of tracks down Main Cross Street did not necessarily determine or change the distribution of residential, commercial, and industrial structures, because these patterns had been unfolding for some time. The streetcar did contribute to the extension of the business section all along its route and stimulated the building or remodeling of business houses. It probably also, as in other cities, had a hand in creating a congested downtown.

The flurry of building activity in Madison in the late 1860s and early 1870s was reminiscent of that which took place twenty years earlier. Among the many manufacturers who relocated, remodeled, or constructed factory buildings during this time, none received as much attention as Richard Johnson and John Clements, the city's leading starch producers. In 1862 Johnson and Clements, as partners, purchased the Madison Watt Starch Factory, situated on Walnut Street just beyond the corporate limits. In 1873 the partnership dissolved, and each man set up plants on the southwest side between the Marine Railway company shipyards and the railroad bend. Clements bought the old Madison Pearl Starch building, essentially rebuilt the factory in stone and brick, and constructed a substantial levee. Clements also rejuvenated a line of cottages north of the factory on Second Street west of McIntyre Street for his employees. His ex-associate meanwhile erected a

EARLY PHOTOGRAPH OF MADISON'S WEST END, showing the huge riverside factory buildings of the starch manufacturers.

Indiana Historical Society

mammoth complex on the site of the old Palmetto Mills, which had burned in 1858. Johnson's new starch factory, designed by John Temperly, was claimed to be the world's third largest. The main building covered almost one acre. Temperly divided the first floor rooms with iron pillars rather than with brick walls. On the second floor he enclosed the proprietor's office with glass so operations could be overseen from one room. Worked into the Vermont slate roof was the Johnson and Son trade name, a feature said to have been visible several miles away. Directly behind the factory was a "village" of corn houses laid off in blocks and called Johnsonville. In 1878 Johnson had telephone lines, Madison's first, installed from his office to the railroad depot and to his home.[132]

130. Madison *Daily Courier,* 22 August 1873, 27 August 1873, 5 September 1873, 6 May 1874, 16 May 1874, 13 June 1874.

131. See for example David R. Goldfield and Blaine A. Brownell, *Urban America from Downtown to No Town* (Boston: Houghton Mifflin Co., 1979), 144–45, 206.

132. Madison *Daily Courier,* 4 May 1868, 3 December 1868, 29 January 1869, 13 June 1873, 27 July 1873, 4 August 1873, 7 August 1873, 25 October 1873, 20 June 1874, 3 November 1874. See also an undated clipping in the Elvin scrapbook on the Johnson Starch Works. On the telephone see the Madison *Daily Evening Star,* 17 January 1878, 27 February 1878, 8 April 1878.

Residential construction kept pace with that of industry. Although a number of sizable houses went up, striving for an Italianate or French Second Empire composition, the impression is that the majority of work went into the more modest tenement or cottage of frame or brick. The vicinity of Walnut Street north of Main Cross and the western portion of the city were built up the most. Builders continued to be aided by the proliferation of pattern books. One such guide commented on by the *Courier* in 1870 not only contained designs for residences and churches with specimens of molding and brackets, but offered to furnish frame buildings of any size or description and ship them to any part of the country.[133] Alexander White, a Madison contractor, also got into the ready-made house business. He fashioned small wooden cottages, placed them on wheels, and delivered them to the designated lots.[134] Much of the remodeling of homes consisted of replacing pine shingle roofs with the fashionable Vermont slate. Decorative iron fencing was placed around a number of the more elegant homes. Several firms sold imported ironwork from Louisville and elsewhere, but much of it was produced at home. The foundry of Cobb, Stribling and Company, founded in 1863, did a land office business in Madison and elsewhere with its patented iron fence that did not require the usual stone underpinning. Wat N. Brown patented an iron fence design and built a shop to manufacture it. John Barrett, a downtown blacksmith, also made iron fencing.[135]

Business houses received comparatively greater consideration from builders than homes or factories, particularly along Main Cross Street. Between 1870 and 1878, but primarily in the earlier years, most merchants either remodeled or rebuilt their estab-

lishments. Whether constructing a new building or revamping an old one, the merchants shared a desire to identify with prevailing commercial architecture. Thus many of the storekeepers chose to modernize their establishments with cast-iron fronts, metal columns, window caps and cornices, along with street-level, plate-glass showcases. More economical than masonry, quicker to put up and dismantle, and available in an array of simulated Classical designs and stone imitations, the modular cast-metal ornamentation was adopted along main streets throughout the land. In Madison the iron fronts were most often imported through local agents from Bourlier and Brothers or from Snead and Company of Louisville. Window caps and cornices were produced in Madison by John Adams, who in 1871 put on his new building the first galvanized sheet-iron cornice made in the city. John Eckert also manufactured and installed cornices.[136]

Not everyone chose to face a building with metal. Brick and carved-stone fronts remained valid options. Some parties changed their minds as to what kind of facing to employ. The Masons' new "French Renaissance" style building ("now so popular in our cities") initially was to have an iron front, according to the design of architect A. M. Connett, but ended up with a stone facade.[137] Perhaps to Masons and to others the ironwork was little more than a cheap counterfeit. Vinton A. Matthews, a carpenter, elected to adorn his residence with a wooden cornice.

133. Madison *Daily Courier*, 29 July 1870.
134. Madison *Daily Evening Star*, 10 May 1877.
135. Madison *Daily Courier*, 15 October 1870, 9 May 1873, 14 June 1873.
136. Ibid., 16 March 1871, 18 April 1871, 29 July 1871; Madison *Weekly Citizen*, 20 December 1873.
137. Madison *Daily Courier*, 4 June 1870, 27 September 1870.

The papers noted that he "put up a solid wood cornice instead of a sham moulding."[138]

Most of the roofs on Madison's business houses were flat or low to medium gabled. The Masonic Hall, and a few other structures styled in French Second Empire, featured the steeply sloped mansard roof covered with multi-colored, shaped slate tiles. Slate, because of its attractiveness, uninflammability, and permanence, was almost universally adopted by Madison's builders. Slate roofing earned a solid endorsement when, for example, the First National Bank and the Madison Insurance Company reroofed their respective buildings with the laminated rock. Slate combined with a mansard roof, however, was not accorded the same enthusiasm. Here the waterproof slate covered an unusual density of parched timber making for disaster if fire should occur. The *Courier* expressed the problem succinctly: "Mansard roofs are nice things for fires. A mass of wood-work, dry as a cinder, covered externally with slate or metal as if intended to be impervious to water, render fire engines perfectly harmless."[139] The paper took special note of the refusal of one of the local fire houses to replace its roof with a mansard design.[140] Nevertheless, the mansard roof had benefits. It added to a building another serviceable level, and one garbed in elegant dress. Thus, the mansard roof and the iron fronts, to take just two examples, exhibited both imposing ornamentation and sensible application, qualities loved by Victorian Americans.

A repetition of design in iron fronts came about as neighboring store owners borrowed ideas from one another or created a commercial block by erecting a common cornice. Such regularity may have appeared aesthetically weak to romantics, but to shop owners it expressed standardization and mechaniza-tion, emerging norms in an industrializing society. On the other hand, a building's individuality attracted customers. This could be variously achieved in an age of malleable iron, of large plate-glass show windows, and of images or graphics hawking a store's specialties. Having the tallest building could accomplish the same objective. Madison's business houses were generally limited to three floors. The variable had to be the height of each level. Thus when G. M. Brooke built his iron front "Trade Palace" in 1867, he elevated the second and third stories several feet above the standard. He then surmounted the top course with an arched centerpiece, making the whole some eighteen feet taller than any other downtown building.[141] Despite efforts to individualize structures the overall effect of the streetscape was, and is, that of a cohesive design characterized by relatively

MADISON FROM THE KENTUCKY SHORE, c. 1880s.

Flora Collection, Indiana State Library

138. Madison *Evening Courier*, 31 October 1874.
139. Madison *Daily Courier*, 13 November 1872.
140. "A new roof is to be placed on the No. 3's fine engine house. It won't be a mansard though." Ibid., 18 October 1870.
141. Ibid., 26 July 1867.

uniform height, the rhythm of capped windows, and heavy projecting cornices.

Madison's building impetus of the early 1870s reflected the prosperous state of the national economy. An upturn proportionally less than that of the 1850s, it nonetheless helped to stabilize for a few years Madison's shrinking business. Other influences besides that of the country's well-being also contributed to the upsurge in construction. Talk of new railroad connections carried weight in the manufacturing sector. The prospect of the Cumberland and Ohio Railroad connecting Chattanooga, Tennessee, to a point opposite Madison directly accounts for several factories being built or expanded, as did the anticipated Ohio River Railroad linking Cincinnati with New Albany.[142] Fire damage inspired the building of new and modern structures. Conflagrations in the spring of 1870 and 1871, for example, wiped out businesses on Main Cross Street, including most of the block between West and Mulberry streets.[143] As important as anything else to the growth of the more economical mid-sized domestic house was the advent of building and loan associations. Begun in Pennsylvania in 1831, the institution proliferated after the Civil War. It was set up expressly to help its shareholders purchase or erect a house, refurbish a home, or start a business. The German Building and Aid Association, established in 1871, was the first institution of this type in Madison. Three years later a total of eight had been incorporated, and many houses had been financed. As the *Weekly Citizen* observed in 1873: "These societies do a great deal to build up a city."[144]

The auspicious flowering of trade unfortunately could not be sustained. Long-term statewide shifts in population, commerce, and transportation probably

BIRD'S EYE VIEW OF MADISON, 1887.
Indiana Historical Society

bear the ultimate responsibility for Madison's subsequent distress. Closer to home, though, the envisioned railroads did not materialize, and without them little could be done to strengthen Madison's industrial position. In addition, the 1873 stock market panic, which set off economic difficulties around the country, severely curtailed the output of Madison's existing factories. In late 1873 the city's major manufacturers were operating on reduced time and workforce schedules, a situation that lasted well into 1875.[145] A brief spurt of activity in the late seventies and early eighties could not mend the

142. See for instance ibid., 24 March 1865, 1 May 1866, 2 November 1866, 8 July 1869, 4 August 1869.

143. Ibid., 23 May 1871, 1 June 1871.

144. Madison *Weekly Citizen*, 13 September 1873. For a discussion of the history and workings of building and loan associations see David P. Handlin, *The American Home Architecture and Society 1815–1915* (Boston: Little, Brown and Co., 1979), 237–43.

145. Madison *Weekly Citizen*, 8 November 1873, 15 November 1873; Madison *Democrat*, 16 January 1875.

damage. Madison's population count began a fifty-year descent from a peak of 10,709 in 1870 to a low of 6,530 in 1930.

After the boom subsided, the city reposed in relative seclusion fostered by its topography and economic stagnation. Immune to the passage of years, for the most part, was its architecture. Today, thanks to the city's lengthy hiatus in construction and subsequent preservation efforts, most of the buildings remain as they were built. They are monuments to the skill and ingenuity of the many carpenter-builders and the few trained architects who created them. They built well, and their legacy to future generations has made Madison a national treasure.

Robert M. Taylor, Jr.

Architectural Details

MADISON'S ARCHITECTURE has been greatly affected by the availability of building materials. The area supplied enormous amounts of yellow poplar, wild cherry, oak, and other trees; hillsides of limestone for quarrying; stream beds filled with limestone ready to be picked up and used; clay banks for brick making; and also iron foundries for making iron fronts, fences, and balconies.

After wood, brick was the favorite construction material, and houses or stores in the early days often had their own brick kilns. These small kilns were not very efficient. Bricks toward the middle might be well fired, but those at the perimeter would be inadequately baked and therefore soft. It was customary to use these soft bricks for interior walls, reserving the hard-fired ones for the exteriors. Some buildings constructed with greater opulence used brick from Cincinnati or Louisville. Occasionally, bricks were hand-polished at the time they were laid. When this was done, small boxes were constructed of boards, possibly three feet long, a foot wide, and a few inches high. Brick dust was then sprinkled in these boxes, and bricks, one by one, were pushed forward and back by hand to acquire a smooth, polished surface which when exposed to the weather would shed water and keep the wall dry.

Throughout the nineteenth century France was considerably ahead of America in the manufacture of window glass. At that time the making of window glass was a handcraft. The rolling process had not yet been established. Window glass was blown in a large bubble at the end of a long blowpipe. This bubble was allowed to elongate until it assumed a tubular shape, which when sufficiently cooled was allowed to rest on a marble-top table. After further cooling, the ends of the tube were sheared off, and the remaining tube was split down the middle with shears, allowing the loose ends to fold back and lie flat on the table. The resulting glass was what we still see today in old windows with wavy surfaces which distort the view. France was able to make larger panes than could be made in this country in the early part of the nineteenth century. So it is possible to assume that glass panes in large sizes were imported from France. Measurements of the panes in the Shrewsbury house (12¾ inches x 25⅝ inches) indicate that the glass probably originated in France. Conversely, the smaller panes in the Sullivan house indicate American orgin.

Putty for installing window glass into the window sash was made on the spot. The procedure was simple. White lead and linseed oil were mixed to the proper consistency, and the resulting putty became as hard as stone when set in a window. Removal of the putty from a sash where window glass had been broken was very difficult, almost impossible, because the putty was so much harder than the wood to which it was attached. However, when heated with a hot iron, it became soft and readily removable.

Another building material that was particularly

valuable was yellow poplar. There was so much of it in this area that at one time it was thought to be inexhaustible. Extravagance and wastefulness occurred. When a big house was being built, it was quite normal to have a bonfire blazing alongside, and every stick of lumber that was not absolutely perfect went on the bonfire. The same was true of cherry lumber. Great cherry trees were utilized with the utmost extravagance. The cherry handrail in the Shrewsbury house staircase, when looked at by a professional lumberman at one time, was found to have been cut in part from a cherry log twenty-nine inches in diameter from sap to sap.

"Appalachian pine," which was brought down river in rafts of logs and sawed after it reached Madison, was also important in construction. "Appalachian pine" was a misnomer because the tree never grew in the Appalachian end of Pennsylvania but came from the Pittsburgh area. This was a fine, hard, straight-grained wood, so hard that after 137 years the floor boards in the Shrewsbury house still show marks of the plane that was used to smooth them after they were laid.

The stone in the hills around Madison is limestone, as is that in the creek beds. Much building stone came from quarries near the hilltops along the river. They supplied lintels and sills for windows and doors. Foundations were frequently laid with stone from creek beds which was easily worked and used in the rough.

Fine building stone was also brought from Portsmouth, Ohio, a place where the Ohio River had cut through a stratum of sandstone. John Patton, former Indiana State Geologist, points out that this is the only place in the world where this particular stratum comes to the surface.[1] Portsmouth sandstone is much harder than the oolitic limestone of Indiana. A great deal of the sandstone was brought to Madison by barges and was used in the building of such structures as the Sullivan, Talbott-Hyatt, and Shrewsbury houses.

There is a vast literature on the design and making of nails. At this point it is important only to state that the nails in the Sullivan house and other buildings of its period were handmade.

Roofing materials were of various kinds. Shingles on the Sullivan house were hard maple, sawed with a taper at random widths. Such maple shingles were widely used at this time. A material that was found on roofs in the middle of the nineteenth century was sheet iron more than a quarter of an inch thick and as large as eight by ten feet. It was said to have come from a factory in Kentucky. Thin sheet-metal roofs with standing seams became very popular and are still to be found on many buildings. Another popular roofing was slate, either in plain color or in two-color designs. A roofer of long experience reports that in his youth slate was bought in lots of five or six carloads a year. It came from Bangor, Maine. Other reports indicate that at a much earlier period slate was brought to the Ohio from the northeastern corner of Pennsylvania.

Lime mortar was strangely lacking in early Madison, despite the fact that the limestone cliffs and clam shells in great quantity were nearby and would have made fine mortar. Instead of lime mortar the builders used mud mixed with beef hair. The Sullivan house has all of its inner walls laid up in this manner. The fireplace wall in the basement kitchen has mud mortar except at the very surface.

Plaster walls were whitewashed up through the

1. From letter of John B. Patton, State Geologist, to John T. Windle, Historic Madison, Inc., July 16, 1976.

first third of the nineteenth century or even later. The whitewash was of a lime base and sometimes carried a small bit of color. In the spring walls were given a new coat of whitewash, and spring housecleaning was over. By the 1840s, when the Lanier and Shrewsbury houses were built, plaster walls were being painted.

Some copper was used, particularly in church steeples and the gutters of public buildings. The steeple at St. Michael's is copper. The old roof and gutters on the courthouse were copper until it was remodeled some years ago. The gutters on the jail, however, had no metal in them. The walls of the jail were laid up with enormous stones, some of them as big as bathtubs, and the top course was hollowed out to make a gutter for rain. That gutter had no liner of any kind.

Sheffield silver brought from England was used to ornament some of the fences and entrances, including the Sullivan house and the Shrewsbury house and several others.

Iron provided both an important aspect of Madison's architecture and a significant industry for the town. Much of Madison's iron work will be noted in the following chapters under styles. At this point it is only necessary to enumerate and to picture some representative examples. A great amount of iron work, both functional and decorative, has survived in Madison. Many fences, gates, railings, balconies, doorways, iron porches, and entire fronts of stores still exist, and they make up a large part of what is now being called the "Madison look."

Noteworthy elements of design include the lyre, the honeysuckle or anthemion, the palmetto form, spear points, curls, and rosettes, some of which are cast and others, wrought. Gates with the Cobb and Stribling fences often show systematized scrolls.

Their posts tend to be heavy and have high bases and frequently show finials at the top. Stribling in 1870 patented a new type of iron fence post which did away with the heavy stone foundation previously used. Examples are to be found on the following properties: Stribling, 625 West Second Street; Friedley-Hoffstadt, 519 and 521 East Main Street; Kirk, 613 West Main Street; Levy-Swarts, 705 West Second Street; Rea, 427 East Main Street.

The earliest surviving Madison directory, 1859, lists four active foundries: Farnsworth, Indiana Foundry (Crawford and Davidson), Jefferson Foundry and Machine Works (Neal), and Madison Foundry. The 1860 business directory lists under foundries: Crawford and Davidson, Dodds and Rutherford, and J. Farnsworth. The 1867 directory lists Indiana Foundry (S. Crawford and Company), Madison Foundry (Cobb, Stribling and Company), and Neal Manufacturing Company. The number of foundries that were active and the span of years covered by their activities indicate a vast amount of work being done. Although their chief products seem to have been marine engines for the river boats and stoves and fences, all probably produced their share of ornamental iron. The Madison Machine Company continued its activities at least until 1907 when it was still listed in the city directory. In addition to the products of the local foundries, gates and fences and fronts were brought in from Evansville and Muncie in Indiana; Cincinnati, Fenton, and Columbus in Ohio; and Louisville, Kentucky.

Finally, many buildings have cornices and window caps of ornamental pressed metal made to simulate stone. Numerous examples are described and illustrated in the Italianate section. The following illustrations serve as additional examples.

Shrewsbury house   *HABS/HAER*

Iron Fence

Lanier house *German Collection*

708 East Main   *Lee Burns*

412 Broadway   *Frank S. Baker*

Iron Porch and Railing

Talbott-Hyatt house   *German Collection*

Iron Balconies

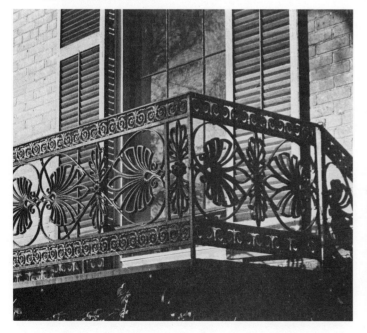

Shrewsbury house   *Frank S. Baker*

306 West Main   *Frank S. Baker*

Iron Balconies and Balustrade

512 East Main *Frank S. Baker*

Lanier house balcony *Lee Burns*

Lanier house balustrade *Lee Burns*

618 West Main   *Frank S. Baker*

Iron Gates and Fences

612 West Main   *Frank S. Baker*

Iron Gates

319 West Second   *German Collection*

403 West First   *German Collection*

Iron Gates (*continued*)

517 West Main   *German Collection*

518 West Second   *German Collection*

419 Broadway   *German Collection*

418 East Second   *Frank S. Baker*

Chamfered Entrances

Broadway Hotel   *Frank S. Baker*

Fourth and Walnut   *Frank S. Baker*

Pressed Metal Details

123 West Main   *German Collection*   223 East Main   *German Collection*

Pressed Metal Details (*continued*)

301-311 West Main   *German Collection*

107 West Main   *German Collection*

107 West Main   *German Collection*

209 East Main   *German Collection*

209 West Main   *German Collection*

218 East Main   *German Collection*

Other Details

Classic doorway, 323 Poplar Street

German Collection

Jefferson County Courthouse window. This window dates
from the period when the courtroom was two stories high.

German Collection

Mausoleum at St. Joseph Cemetery, Classic and Italianate,
1895

German Collection

Italianate derivation with stick decorations in the gable,
506-508 West Second

German Collection

Bracketed Gable Ends

Frank S. Baker

Frank S. Baker

319 West Second *Frank S. Baker*

Frank S. Baker

III

Federal

WITH THE CONCLUSION of the War of Independence and the establishment of the country as a free nation, there emerged a new architectural style, the Federal. Initiated largely by Thomas Jefferson in his effort to develop a fashion for America which would be indigenous to this country, the Federal style was a reaction against the formalism of the Colonial Georgian style which had preceded it. It attempted to serve as a statement of the philosophy and aspirations of the new nation, emphasizing simplicity of design, little ornamentation, symmetry, and studied relationships of openings. The whole effect was one of lightness and harmony.

The Federal style originated in England, where it was known as "Adamesque," named for the English architects James and Robert Adam. It was the Adam brothers, primarily Robert, who originated and developed it, combining the Classic architecture of Greece and Rome with Renaissance and Palladian forms.[1] Robert Adam was interested not only in simplification but in a more delicate system of lines and masses than had been the designers before him. He is credited with being the first person to design a complete interior so that architecture, furniture, draping, and all elements would harmonize. He was particularly opposed to the heaviness of Chippendale, which had suited the Georgian style of Williamsburg so well.

In the Federal period houses were customarily made of brick as they had been in the Colonial Georgian era, but they were taller and not so wide. Wings were often added to the rear rather than to the side. Windows were elongated vertically from the Georgian windows, in which each sash was almost exactly square.

1. John Poppeliers, S. Allen Chambers, and Nancy B. Schwartz, *What Style Is It?* (Washington: The Preservation Press of the National Trust for Historic Preservation, 1977), 12.

1. Sullivan House

The Sullivan house at 304 West Second Street is one of three known Federal structures, the others being the Talbott-Hyatt and the Robinson-Schofield, erected before 1820 on the outskirts of Madison at the present intersection of Second and Poplar streets. Virginia-born Jeremiah Sullivan (1794–1870) came to Madison in 1816 to practice law. He built his home in 1818 and from this base went on to carve an esteemed career as state legislator, state supreme court judge and county judge, Presbyterian elder, and Mason. He helped found Hanover College and the Indiana Historical Society.

Of the three neighboring houses, Sullivan's has undergone the fewest alterations. It exhibits Federal elements that might be seen today in Georgetown, Washington, D.C.: the brick exterior, the cubic main block, a rear wing, a simply ornamented cornice, tall windows, delicate tapered and reeded columns between the entrance door and sidelights, and an elliptical fanlight. Various Georgian elements of design have held over from the eighteenth century, for example, the twin chimneys which stand at the top of the east wall of the main block of the house. Side galleries such as those on the rear wing had been especially popular in the Carolinas, Maryland, and Virginia. They are interesting here because they show so clearly how the early settlers brought with them the ideas of architecture with which they were already familiar.

Most of the materials used in the construction of the house were obtained locally. The foundation stone, laid up with lime mortar in the exterior walls and adobe in the inside walls, probably came from nearby Telegraph Hill, where the outcrop was easily accessible. The color and texture are very similar, if not identical, to the surface rock still visible on the hill just east of town. Not locally acquired were the front steps made of sandstone from Portsmouth, Ohio, and the delicate iron railing, probably a Cincinnati product imported from that city's, and the region's, first iron foundry, established in 1817.

The roof of the main block is two-pitch, while that on the wing is a camelback with the comb at the west wall and the gutter at the east wall. The shingles were originally hand-rived maple. Unusual bricks on the

Joe Scheirich

Dining room as restored and furnished by Historic Madison, Inc.

HABS/HAER

Entrance   *Joe Scheirich*

Side galleries   *HABS/HAER*

front facade exhibit a lower lip which reduces the exposure of mortar to inclement weather. The extreme weight and massiveness of the hardware on the outside doors is characteristic of the period, as are the small brass knobs on the inside doors. The outside woodwork is largely original, although the side galleries have sustained considerable restoration. Some of the handrails, spindles, and posts are recent as is the beaded ceiling on the lower gallery. The often whitewashed ceiling rafters of the upper gallery, long concealed by a false ceiling, are once again exposed.

The Sullivan house is an example of an asymmetrical form in Federal-style structures. Instead of a central hall, it has a broad stairhall to one side of the house flanked by two rooms, with only the front room facing the street. Originally a small door connected the two rooms, which were used probably in the manner of the day, the front room for formal occasions and the back room for family activities. Sullivan, for a time, may have used the rear room with its side porch entrance as a study and law office. Between 1880 and 1890 large machine-made doors replaced the small door, apparently in an effort to follow the fashion for a double parlor. The second floor contains two bedrooms over the parlors with two additional rooms in the wing. The third floor, above the main block of the house, provided space for a schoolroom for the Sullivan children who were taught by their mother. This room was restored by Historic Madison, Inc., in 1983, to reflect its original purpose.

Sullivan put a basement under the entire house. Most of his neighbors had one small basement room, none at all, or depended on covered storage pits. Sullivan's basement had at least six rooms and provided storage space, workrooms, and a kitchen. Some of the inner walls were laid up with stone and others with soft brick. All of them were laid in adobe. The adobe was of local yellow clay mixed with beef hair. A thin coat of whitewash was brushed on the surface and served to hold the clay in place. The same adobe served as the ground coat of the plaster throughout the house, both on brick walls and on the split-hickory laths. The large basement room under the side gallery held the winter supply of wood for the fireplaces. The stairs leading from this room into the backyard still retain the original, wide outside door and hardware.

Food was prepared in the main kitchen in the basement. The kitchen floor was half paved with brick; the other half was probably tamped earth. The huge fireplace of stone, laid up with river mud with a thin finish of lime mortar on the surface, has the original iron bars supporting the arch and a wood mantelshelf. The brick hearth is original. The windows in the kitchen, like all the basement windows, are above ground, but are larger than the others as a result of being set in pits for admitting more light. The vertical iron bars at all basement windows were a security measure. The handrail and spindles of the basement stairs are thought to be original because of the method of construction. The spindles are mortised into the handrail at an angle, without a nail, characteristic of carpentry methods of that era.

Food was brought up the narrow stairs into the serving kitchen at the back of the main floor where it was transferred from cooking utensils to fine china. The china was washed in this room and returned to the dish cupboards; it would never have been taken to the cooking kitchen below. A cistern near the back door supplied the water heated at the fireplace in the serving kitchen. Probably the hot water carried to the bedrooms came from this source.

The woodwork in the house, which was always painted, has survived in remarkably fine condition and reflects the work of the English cabinetmaker, Thomas Sheraton. Sheraton was strongly influenced by Robert Adam, and while Sheraton was chiefly active in the 1780s and 1790s, his designs were copied or adapted in the Middle West throughout the first third of the nineteenth century. The reeded woodwork is directly derived from Sheraton. The fireplace mantles show the influence of Adam but display modifications from other sources. The turned lips just under the shelves indicate a Dutch derivation. The house's chair rails are all in place; the cornices are original. The floors, made of pit-sawed, random ash boards, are in their original state. Inside doors are all handmade, wood-pinned, and mortised, with the exception of the large doors between the two parlors. Except for the ash floors and the maple shingles, the wood throughout the house is poplar. The staircase, with its simple turned cherry handrail and square spindles, is almost identical with one at the Winterthur Museum in Wilmington, Delaware.

The Sullivan smokehouse and useable bake oven, accurately reconstructed in 1985–86 on the Poplar Street side of the property, is an example of the usual aggregation of service rooms and buildings extending the full depth of the lot behind the main house. These features can still be found on many properties in Madison. Outbuildings usually included stables for horses and occasionally for a cow since the public milk supply was late in coming. A comment to the effect that droves of pigs being driven to the river for shipping lost several of their numbers in transit through the city streets seems to indicate the existence of various service buildings where they could be concealed. Every house had to have storage for fuel:

coal, wood, kindling, and ashes. Many houses still show a group of rooms which were unquestionably for these uses. Frequently the service buildings included living rooms for some of the help, though often help lived down the streets in their own houses and worked by the day. These outbuildings did not necessarily follow the design of the main house, although in some instances they were designed as fully as the house itself.

Considered Madison's finest Federal-style mansion, the endangered Sullivan house was purchased by Historic Madison, Inc., in 1961, restored, and dedicated in 1963.

2. Talbott-Hyatt House

At least a portion of the Talbott-Hyatt house,[2] 301 West Second Street, was built prior to January 19, 1819. Richard C. Talbott advertised in a Madison

Ward's Studio

2. In *Indiana Houses of the Nineteenth-Century* (Indianapolis: Indiana Historical Society, 1962), Wilbur Peat refers to the house as the Allison-Hyatt house. However, according to deed records Allison did not own the property until 1867.

paper on this date for the rental of "three well furnished rooms, in his brick house, on the corner of second and poplar streets."[3] A veteran of the War of 1812, Talbott came to Madison around 1814 from Pennsylvania. He held several Jefferson County offices before again entering military service, this time giving his life for the American cause against Mexico in the late 1840s.

The house is basically Federal in style with only a slight cornice and close-clipped roof at the gable ends, chimneys within the walls, and windows that are six over six. It was built in stages. Internal evidence reveals that the first portion, made of brick, consisted of one room on the first floor, the present east bay of the living room, a room about fourteen feet square with a room above and a basement below. On the south side an open wooden porch extended from both levels connected by a wooden staircase. Eventually the porch was enclosed with brick to make halls, and the old staircase was replaced by the present one. An outside staircase with batten doors led from the basement to the garden at ground level. The entrance to the house was on Poplar Street (formerly Poplar Lane) and still survives. Portsmouth, Ohio, quarries furnished the stone for the steps. The wrought iron railing is almost identical to that at the Sullivan house, and it probably came from the same Cincinnati foundry. The horizontal window and the door, both with colored glass panes, are Victorian additions.

A separate kitchen was also put up when the original corner room was built. The kitchen porch appears to have been built at two different times. Initially erected was a first floor porch with a slanted roof; afterwards a porch was added above, which was partly enclosed with large wood louvers. The floor of this second level porch still slants because it was laid

Kitchen fireplace   *John T. Windle*

on the original rafters of the first floor porch.

Talbott's notice of three furnished rooms to rent indicates that more than just the two-room main block and kitchen was in place before 1819. One theory is that an unattached brick wing, no longer standing, was built west of the kitchen shortly after the initial construction. In 1965 an archaeologist, supplied by James H. Kellar, former professor of archaeology and director of the Glenn A. Black Laboratory at Indiana University, excavated the foundations of this west wing and had drawings made, which are now filed at the Shrewsbury house. The wing comprised a large room on the first floor with an equally large room above it with brick chimneys in the center. A full basement was accessible by an outside brick staircase. An open space of some three feet existed between the two buildings. After measurements and photographs were taken, the excavation was refilled in the belief that such foundations are best preserved when covered.

The primary well on the property still exists, though concealed by a flat stone. It is located near the southwest corner of the main house and illustrates the early nineteenth-century method of digging wells

3. *Indiana Republican*, 19 January 1819, 23 January 1819, 6 February 1819.

by hand. A circular pit about eleven feet wide and ten feet deep was hollowed out. The dimensions were governed by the ease with which a man could toss dirt over his shoulder and over the rim of the pit with a shovel. The pit was walled with brick or stone. In the middle of the pit a narrow shaft was dug by a small man or boy using a small shovel and a bucket on a rope. This small shaft was also walled with brick or stone and went deep enough to reach water.

In 1853 the price jumped to $10,000, indicating extensive changes just prior to that date and giving credence to the theory that the large front room with its long windows was built about that time. The cap over the Second Street door was fashionable in the 1850s. The windows of the new part reached to the floor, and the street window in the old section was altered to conform. A staircase, not extant, was put at the southwest corner. Old photographs show that the Second Street steps, placed probably when the extension was built, formerly had a wood railing with wood posts. The present leaded glass door set in a frame with a shallow reveal is probably a later substitution. About 1870 an entrance to the basement off Second Street was veneered with stone, and a basement window on the same side of the house was screened with an iron grill.

Subsequent owners of the house included James Y. Allison who held the property from 1867 to 1894, and Benjamin C. Hyatt. In 1962 Virginia Hyatt McBride and her husband, Pierre, of Louisville, Kentucky, deeded the lot to Historic Madison, Inc. Among restoration efforts has been the relaid garden, with authentic plants largely contributed by friends of the project. Historic Madison, Inc., removed, in 1969, a Victorian house that had been built on the west half of the garden site which was pur-

chased in 1895 for that purpose. In 1971 HMI erected a carriage house and stable on the original carriage house foundation. A potting shed was added from designs by A. J. Downing repeatedly published in his magazine, the *Agriculturalist*. The pioneer garden is one of few such attractions in the United States.

3. Schofield House

Lee Burns

The Schofield house, 217 West Second Street, is best known as the site of the organizing of the Grand Lodge of Free Masons of Indiana, which took place here on January 13, 1818.

The house has many of the architectural idioms of the period. The mass of the house is a block facing Second Street with a similar massive block extending to the rear along Poplar Street. An additional block at the south end of this extension on Poplar Street has been added to replace a frame lean-to which in turn replaced a log lean-to. Both were of one story; the current replacement is two stories. The restoration fortunately could be based on an early photograph supplied by Lee Burns, eminent architect and historian (1872–1957).

The cornice is stepped out in two courses of bricks set at an angle. Windows have been returned to six over six on the second level and nine over six on the first level. The first story windows and door facing Second Street are capped by semicircular lunettes made of slightly projecting bricks. The entrance doors are recessed by the depth of the wall. Heavy shutters with louvers have been replaced in their original thickness. A two-pitch roof running north and south covers the west extension and the main block of the house forming a hip with the two-pitch roof running east and west over the front of the house. This east and west roof terminates in a gable facing east. The entrances on Second Street and Poplar Street have been modified and are now cement steps with iron railings. The chimneys have been restored to their original design.

Tradition has it that the large lodge room on the second floor was originally designed to house overnight guests traveling through. They might have been served their meals in the kitchens on the first floor, and tradition also has it that the room under the lodge room was a tavern where there would have been available alcoholic beverages. The corner room is said to have been a store for the sale of fabrics, tinware, and staple groceries.

The question of who built the house has arisen because of less than explicit information supplied by the deed record. One group of interpreters wishes to attribute the building to Alexander Lanier, although his name does not appear at any point in the deed record. Another group would attribute the building to William Robinson, although Robinson's name does not appear on the deed record until 1820, two years after the Masons' organization meeting.

In 1972 the Ancient Accepted Scottish Rite in the Valley of Indianapolis purchased the property from the heirs of the late Mrs. Charlotte Schofield for eventual presentation to the Freemasons of Indiana. It was turned over to the Masonic Heritage Foundation, and extensive restorations were made by H. Roll McLaughlin and Forrest Camplin, architects. The building was opened to the public as a Masonic museum on April 19, 1975, with elaborate ceremonies.

4. Sheets-Lanham House

Ward's Studio

During the heyday of stagecoach travel the rear portion of this house at 703 West Main Street served as a stop on the line where passengers could rest, eat, and spend the night. It was built between 1834 and 1849, probably in the earlier part of that period, by the Sheets family, which owned extensive properties in antebellum Madison and operated a dry goods store among other businesses. The rear hostelry was the original part, built in the Federal style. Each level of the two-story inn had two rooms with a large fireplace in each room and a porch on the east side. A staircase connected the porches. The deep basement doubled as a wine cellar.

Most likely the front structure was put up in the

early 1850s. In contrast to its Federal-styled rear building, the streetside dwelling has Classic appointments including plain heavy lintels over the second floor windows and a cornice of brick dentils. Because the ground sloped upward from the rear to the street, the front building was higher than the back unit. Steps, therefore, had to be built at each level between the two sections. Evidence points to this building as having been a store, possibly built for that purpose by John Sheets. The stone stringcourse dividing the first and second levels is found on a number of storefronts. Such horizontal bands were used to bear the weight of upper stories that rested on frames of large show windows. In addition, a break in the low stone foundation shows the existence at one time of a center door. At a later date the center door was walled in, and the entire exterior of the lower level was made over to approximate the design of the upper story. The existing corner door with the sidelights and transom was probably installed at this time.

Henry Pfeiffer and John Lanham were former owners of this building. John L. Richert is the present owner.

5. McKee-Powell House

James McKee was the original owner of this house at 428 Mulberry Street. It was built in a severely plain style, essentially Federal, by Matthew Temperly, an important Madison architect-builder. Before moving to Indianapolis in 1832, Temperly lived for five years in Baltimore and presumably received architectural training there. Since the date of construction of the McKee house is 1832, it may have been Temperly's first professional commission in Madison and the

Robert Twente

Photograph showing house before 1930

Lee Burns

reason for his removal from Indianapolis to Madison in 1833. He died in 1861 at age 56.

The house was built to the sidewalk on two sides and originally had a garden wall stretching along Third Street from the house to the alley. Extensive remodeling later in the century lengthened the street windows to the floor and added an Italianate cornice across the top. In the early 1930s Edward D. James further remodeled the house by putting the Classic columns at the doorway and panels and iron grills at the bottom of the long street windows. He also removed the Italianate cornice, returning to the early brick dentils. A two-story porch appears at the rear in the ell of the house. Former owner Leslie White installed the sidewalk showcases. Anna G. Powell was another former owner of the house. The present owner is the Madison Insurance Agency, Inc.

Frank S. Baker

6. Leonard-Distel House

George Leonard, a native of Massachusetts and a prominent Madison merchant, appears to have been the builder of this house at 202 West Second Street. He owned the quarter block from Cherry Lane to the alley to the west. The date of construction has not been determined. If the house was on the property in 1825 when the lot was transferred from one Leonard to another for $100, then the amount of the transaction is difficult to explain. And, unfortunately, the next sale recorded is not until 1857, the year after George Leonard's death. The Federal features of the house hint at an early date of building, possibly in the 1820s.

The house was built in sections and finally reached to the alley at the north. Stables and two-story living quarters for servants once sat on the property, but these structures have long since been sold off. At the entrance the stone steps and iron handrail are similar to those at the Sullivan house, one block away. Windows on the front facade have lintels of wedged brick; those on the sides have lintels of smooth stone. Porches on two levels once faced

the garden toward the west; the upper porch has since been enclosed. The present owners are George E. and Selma Distel.

7. Thurston House

This 1830s Federal brick with brick dentils at 220 Walnut Street has a main block facing the sidewalk with gable ends facing north and south. A long wing toward the back has a two-storied gallery along the south side and a camelback roof comparable to that

Frank S. Baker

on the Sullivan house. The wing's windows are six over six and appear to be original, as does the roof of metal standing seam. The doorway is slightly recessed; the door is a replacement. The reveal on the recess is paneled. The steps of the approach are of native stone. A stone band lies above the foundation of the front facade. The iron rail is decorated with a lyre and includes a suspended iron seat. The loop and spear fence is a recent installation. Nancy Thurston is the present owner.

8. Devenish-Fry-Haigh House

HABS/HAER

Side galleries   *Robert Twente*

Solomon Devenish built the Federal-styled rear part of this house, 108 East Third Street, between 1837 and 1839. The front section, set on the higher ground level, was erected by William H. Fry in a mixed style, with cornice elements that are late Classic. Fry came to Madison in 1849 and opened a coal distributorship at the corner of Ohio and Main streets, now Vaughn Drive and Jefferson Street. By 1851 he was in partnership with John Maxwell selling iron. Later Fry and Maxwell joined with J. P. Walker as "Salt agents, commission merchants and dealers in iron, nails, steel, castings, blacksmith tools, axles, springs, woodwork, etc."[4]

Fry probably supplied the iron benches on his house and the house next door. These iron seats are infrequently found, but at times seen in Baltimore and Philadelphia houses of the period. The door from the porch to the kitchen is Dutch, in that the top half is hinged separately from the bottom half. The same double hinging occurs in the front section of the house where a shutter is divided so that the top swings free of the bottom.

Rachel Haigh owned the house at a later date. Opal Hines is the present owner.

4. U.S. Department of the Interior, Report of John Hopkins, historian, for the Historic American Buildings Survey, no. In-125, 1978.

Iron benches   *German Collection*

9. McClain-Park House

Sharing a common wall with the Devenish house is the two-story brick at 106 East Third Street that originally belonged to William McClain. More than likely it was built in the 1830s, and it exhibits both Federal and Classic elements. Both the east and west end walls have fractables carried above the roof with bridged chimneys incorporated in the Federal manner. The windows and the doorway are topped by wedged brick lintels, also found in the Classic style. The four steps are dressed stone, the lower one being a curtail shape. The iron benches, though probably supplied by neighbor William Fry, are of a different design than those on the Devenish porch.

A very large kitchen with cooking fireplace in addition to a large wine cellar once occupied the basement. Moody Park, one of Madison's early residents who established a cotton mill in the 1820s and became Madison's first mayor (1838–50), purchased this house in 1866. It remained in his family for many years. The property is now the possession of Lawrence and Joyce Schaefer.

Robert Twente

10. Main Street Row Houses

Like the Devenish and McClain houses, the buildings at 710–14 East Main Street are side by side, but the latter are defined as row houses because there are three living units instead of two connected with common walls. These row houses were probably built in 1838. The tax record of 1837 fails to note the buildings or their owners. The tax record of 1838 is missing, but that for the following year, 1839, lists two of the three buildings. Internal evidence indicates that all three houses were constructed at the same

Robert Twente

time. They were owned by Philip Pfaff, George Wehrle, and John Marx. John McIntyre laid out additions to the east of town, including the section on which these houses were built. A native of Baltimore, McIntyre was a wealthy landowner and merchant who came to Madison around 1814 after a brief business experience in Cincinnati. Influenced by the architectural styles of his native city, McIntyre likely was responsible for the naming of Baltimore Street in 1840 in this eastside area.

The walls are made of rubble, small stones set together in mortar. Forms were fabricated and filled with the rubble and mortar, tamped and pounded to remove air bubbles. The surface of the front facade was given a smooth coat of stucco and then marked with a trowel to imitate cut stone. Halfway between the upper and lower windows is a protruding belt band. The eaves overhang, and the stucco cornice projects slightly.

The front windows exhibit an interesting design. The window frames and glazing are flush with the exterior surface of the wall. The window openings curve in at the sides, a vertical curve making an embrasure that is wider on the interior than it is on the outside of the house. A single vertical muntin divides each sash into two glass panels. This practice was not common prior to the 1850s, so the large panes probably replace earlier, smaller ones. The window on the west has small panes, six over six, which are apparently original. Shutters appear on all windows.

The east house in this row has a cooking fireplace in the basement with a wood mantle and a wide aperture to accommodate the cooking utensils. It also has a circular cistern, a drum of masonry rising from the basement floor so that the water is contained in a sort of tank. Though the backs of the three houses have been extensively altered, Historic Madison, Inc., received an easement to the facades from Charles and Nancy Farnsley in 1984, giving the organization authority over any future changes to the facades.

Robert Twente

11. Jefferson Street Row Houses

These row houses in the 500 block of Jefferson Street, made of brick and joined by common walls, were possibly erected between 1835 and 1839, at the time the buildings in the 300 block of Jefferson Street were constructed. The style is mixed, merging from the Federal into the Classic, with Classic smooth-cut window lintels and brick dentils in the cornice. The recessed doorways are a Classic influence. Bridged chimneys flank the comb of the roof and are a return to an earlier Georgian era. Some of the windows are multi-paned originals, while the one over one lights are obvious replacements. Several of the roofs appear to be original metal with standing seams, and several of the common walls project above the roofline and are stepped.

HABS/HAER

12. Baltimore Row

These Federal-style buildings at 408–414 East Third Street are sometimes referred to as the Baltimore Row because they represent a strong influence from the East Coast. They may have been put on the lots before the 1840s during the ownership of Isaac Eudaily or John Low (or Lowe).[5] The houses are two rooms deep, with storeroom and kitchen in the basement, double parlors on the first floor, two bedrooms on the second floor, and two more in the attic. The gable attic dormers are holdovers from eighteenth-century architecture. The cornice is almost nonexistent, and the window lintels are smooth stone with blocks at the ends. Most of the windows have been modified, but some of the early six over six still exist. A tunnel at a dividing wall covers a walkway from the street to the back of the house. This device can be found in buildings around town that are built with common walls.

5. In his M.A. thesis, "A History of Jefferson County, Indiana" (Indiana University, 1932), 60, Emery O. Muncie discusses the large number of Baltimorians who came to Madison.

Robert Twente

13. Broadway Row Houses

These row houses at 503–509 Broadway demonstrate a mixture of stylistic elements, including brick dentils in the second house from the left, a style which appeared in Madison between 1835 and 1839, or earlier. The Italianate cornices on houses three and four are identical and were added at a later date. House number 503 (left in the picture) has a more elaborate cornice and window caps, and a hooded door cap, all of which unquestionably represent subsequent remodeling. The smooth, flush window caps on the second and fourth houses from the left suggest the retention of a previous style. Two of the houses have a runway between them, entered by an arched opening in the continuous street wall. The third and fourth houses from the left were probably built about 1838, and the other two houses between 1840 and 1850.

Jesse Bright, William Ford, and John Sangree were the first owners of the property. Jonathan and Stephanie Smith are the present owners of 503 and 505, while Anna Laura Peddie is the owner of 507 and 509.

14. Bright and Mersdorff Houses

From simple beginnings in the Federal style these two houses at 310 and 312 West Third Street bear the stamp of subsequent modernizing in the Italianate style, particularly noticeable in the wide eaves supported by large brackets, and in the window caps on the house at the left. A portion of this house, however, was built in 1822 by William Brown and was the first brick house west of Broadway.[6]

Robert Twente

The cornice of the house at 312 (left) contains modillions and dentils with heavy brackets at the corners. The chimneys are bridged and indicate a stylistic holdover from Georgian chimneys. The cornice of the outer framing of the entrance is arched in the Palladian manner. The recessed door is a recent alteration. Jesse Bright (1812–1875) was a later owner of this house. Bright served in the state

6. Madison *Evening Courier*, 31 October 1874.

Frank S. Baker

legislature and in the statehouse as lieutenant governor in 1843. A United States senator beginning in 1845, Bright was expelled from that body in 1862 for having written a letter of introduction for an acquaintance to Jefferson Davis, president of the Confederacy. Henry and Esther Smith now own the Bright house.

The house at 310 West Third Street, probably built in the 1830s, retains the original stone window caps, and the door remains flush with the sidewalk. The windows in the rear and on the sides that have not been modified are six over six and give further evidence of the house having been built during the Federal period. The John Mersdorff family presently owns this house.

15. Federal Group

These three houses at 419, 423, and 425 East Third Street, with stone lintels on regularly spaced windows and doors, serve as good examples of the rhythm so frequently found in the Federal period. They also illustrate the manner in which the Italian influence affected earlier structures. The middle house had Italian ornaments added in the cornice and over the windows and doors at a later date. Window panes in all three houses have been updated.

16. Federal Cottage and Office

The low, one-story brick building, sometimes referred to as a Federal cottage, is illustrated in the structures at 104 East Third Street and 424 West Street. The building at 104 East Third Street, with shuttered windows and smooth lintels, exhibits the mass, outline, and lack of detail of the Federal period. It was constructed before 1841. D. N. Reid, Sr., was an early owner of this building.[7] The present owner is Madison Lodge, B.P.O.E.

The other cottage, 424 West Street, has the thin unornamented cornice and the low-pitched roof commonly found in the Federal style. It also has segmentally arched brick lintels over the doors and windows and four over four panes in the sash. This cottage went up after 1841. Its owner is Anne Wilberding.

Robert Twente

17. Federal Cottage

Another brick Federal cottage is located at 902 West First Street. Probably built around 1837, it has the gallery under the main roof of the house, an architectural design that likely arrived in Madison from the Carolinas by way of Kentucky. It is shown in this house in its simplest form. Each of the three rooms, side by side, has a door opening onto the gallery. There is no ornament; posts rise slim and straight from what was originally a wood floor. The standing seam roof appears to be original. Lue Ollie White is the present owner.

Frank S. Baker

7. Madison *Daily Courier*, 26 August 1885.

Frank S. Baker

Frank S. Baker

18. Banta House

The stone house on Highway 7 at the Middle Fork bridge, about six miles north of Madison, is an example of the early Federal style. According to a 1976 letter from John Patton, then Indiana State Geologist, this house may be one of the earliest stone buildings erected in Indiana and may have been put up by Scottish settlers as early as the late 1790s.

The masonry is superbly handled, especially in the chimneys. Patton explains: "The original builder used the western European town house system of dressing the stone on the front facade, and perhaps around the first turn, and of using at least controlled, if not standardized course heights for the front of the building. In contrast, the walls farther back are of the kind that is termed rubble construction, which means rock units of virtually any size or shape set in an excess of mortar."[8] The house has been modified as is apparent in the bargeboard ornamentation and the projecting eaves and gable ends.

The building supposedly served as a station for blacks escaping from the South. It has a cavern under it which can be entered only by diving into a pool of water and coming up inside the cavern. Anna O. Banta was a later owner of the house. The present owners are Robert and Kathleen Knoebel.

19. Bachman-Davis House

Another early stone house is located on Highway 56, one-half mile east of the city. It too is reputed to be one of the earliest stone houses in Indiana and a station on the underground railroad. Undocumented tradition has it that this building, containing two rooms, one down and one up, was erected by two brothers who ran a ferry. Later a tollgate was placed at this point on the road. Chapman Harris, an ex-slave preacher, farmer, and blacksmith, occupied the house when it was on the underground railroad. Harris is said to have done his blacksmith work at night and used his hammer and anvil to signal to people in Kentucky when it was safe to bring slaves across the river. Alois Bachman owned this property from 1825 until the partition of his estate in 1887. James and Stella Davis bought it in 1909. It was sold by the Davis family to Dealton Bennett who now owns it.

8. From letter of John B. Patton, State Geologist, to John T. Windle, Historic Madison, Inc., July 16, 1976.

HABS/HAER

Frank S. Baker

20. Gatekeeper's House-Madison State Hospital

Originally a gatekeeper's house on the road to Indianapolis, this stone house on Cragmont Street (Highway 7) at the east gate of the Madison State Hospital is now a property of the hospital. Built around the late 1830s, the original Federal-style stone house had two rooms, one above the other. Porches were added probably about 1910 and one-story additions to the rear were added then or subsequently. The structure was connected with the main highway after 1837 by a footbridge over the railroad track. The half-timbering is recent. Although Federal when built, the disfigurements have completely concealed its original style.

21. Mulberry Street Block

This group of buildings on the west side of Mulberry Street, in the 300 block between Main and Second streets, may have been constructed as early as 1819. The block, therefore, contains some of the town's older Federal-styled buildings, many retaining their original facades. The buildings were remodeled from time to time, and traces of the cast-iron fronts, put on in the 1860s and later, remain. Most of the structures are three stories. The only two-story building is south of the alley and was once Pardy's restaurant. Jeremiah Sullivan owned the building while he lived at the corner of Second and Poplar streets. A notice in the *Indiana Republican* of July 10, 1819, announced that he had moved his office to an upper room of the new brick tenement of Doctor Canby on Mulberry Street and that he would constantly attend the Jennings, Ripley, and Clark circuit courts. Sullivan purchased the building in 1837 and kept it for twenty years.

The building with the disengaged iron columns at 309 Mulberry Street has a brick denticulated cornice and a cast-iron front on the first floor. The three, quatrefoil cast-iron columns with tall bases and

Iron columns at 309 Mulberry   *HABS/HAER*

foliated capitals flank the doorways. The doors are double and may be original. A second door at the south edge functions as an entrance to a stairway to the upper floors. The sills are stone, but the belt band across the front over the doorways has a facing of wood. Windows on the second and third floors have stone sills and undecorated stone caps. The four over four double-hung sashes are probably original. The display windows on the first floor are replacements. A variation occurs in the deeply cut wood panels under the display windows. These panels occur in pairs instead of singles. There are no pilasters at the extremes of the facade.

22. Jefferson Street Row

This row of buildings on the east side of Jefferson Street in the half block north of Second Street is characteristic of the early architecture in Madison that has survived with very little change to the present day. The Federal-style buildings were constructed between 1835 and 1839 or earlier, as in the case of the Farmers and Mechanics' Bank, which occupied the two middle buildings. On June 11, 1817, the bank acquired from John Paul and John McIntyre the

Frank S. Baker

property where 308 and 310 Jefferson Street are today. The entrance with its sidelights of the middle building on the right, now the office of John Ready O'Connor, probably dates from the time of the bank, making this building much earlier than the others on the block.[9] The northernmost building (far left) displays a shallow, undecorated wood cornice; the other three buildings, each a step lower on the street, have brick denticulated cornices.

9. Jefferson County, Deed Records, Book B, 30–31.

Frank S. Baker

23. West Main Street Shops

These brick buildings at 407, 409, and 411 West Main Street provide a good impression of the way Main Street looked in the middle forties. The shed roof toward the street is most characteristic. The buildings at 407 and 409 have denticulated brick cornices. The wedged-brick window caps at 407 place the building within the style of the Federal period. The entrance door is topped by a transom extending across the door and side panels, indicating that the side panels are a replacement of earlier sidelights. The double-hung windows, never replaced by plate glass, are very early. The present owners, Claude and Rebecca Routon, uncovered the date 1836 painted on a piece of metal at the top of the downspout on the left corner of 407. That could well be the date of construction. That the building at 409 was built at a different time is indicated by a seam in the masonry. The stone window lintels at 409 again indicate a somewhat later time of building.

The building at 411, taller and probably somewhat later, gable end toward the street, has larger windows upstairs and down, and the ones on the first floor are replacements. The windows on the second floor have stone lintels, and the ones on the first floor are topped by a stone band across the face of the building. Brick dentils occur above the upper windows below the pediment of the gable end.

24. Lotz-Greves Building

According to local records this stately three-story brick business house at 306 West Main Street was built sometime between 1817 and 1836. Basically Federal in design, it has received modifications through the years, including the addition of the Italianate cornice. The iron balcony, decorated with the lyre, is typical of balconies on many storefronts on the main street. Also representative of the storefront is the stone stringcourse across the front above the openings. Here the form of the band is a twelve-inch belt surmounted by a slightly projecting four-inch course. Besides the main entrance there is a second entrance to a staircase to the living quarters on the second and third floors.

Robert Twente

Benjamin Branham was the building's first owner, followed by Bernhardt Lotz. The present owners, Ronald and Evangeline Greves, on October 8, 1978, granted an easement to Historic Madison, Inc., providing for the preservation of the facade of the building.

25. Broadway Hotel

Werner Braun

Madison has had two Broadway Hotels, practically side by side but in business at different times. The south part of the present Broadway Hotel at 313–17 Broadway, encompassing its entrance with its sidelights and transom, could date from the 1830s. In 1825 John Paul sold to Hannah Buttrick a thirty-foot lot on the west side of Broadway north of the alley between Second and Main Cross streets. Shortly afterwards a building was put on the lot, the south part of the present hotel. In time another structure was erected to the north of the first building. The two buildings had a common wall. The chamfered corner entrance seems to be a Madison Machine Company product and is characteristic of a later phase of Madison architecture. See buildings 121 (Collins-Davee) and 122 (Zeiser-Harrod) for

other examples. By 1905 the buildings were owned by the Finnegan family which had operated saloons in them since 1879. This cluster of buildings became the present Broadway Hotel. The first listing of the Broadway Hotel at the current address appears in the city directory of 1912. An earlier Broadway Hotel, erected just north of the present hotel on the southwest corner of Broadway and Main Cross Street in the 1840s, retained its name until 1903. Eventually this structure was torn down. The present owners of the hotel are Maurice and Peggy Hublar.

26. Hotel Building

The old brick commercial Federal-style building at 402 East Main Street was constructed in 1851 by James Bachman and August L. Frevert. It was used as a hotel for many years beginning as the Indian Kaintuck and subsequently under the names

Frank S. Baker

Bachman, Schwab, and others. When the hotel was offered for sale in 1865 for $7,000 it included twenty-four rooms and an icehouse.[10]

The building is three stories with a denticulated cornice, hip roof, six over six windows with slightly pedimented stone lintels, and a stone band on the Main Street side above the first floor. The store windows may be the originals and have four panes with transoms above and wood panels below. Slightly recessed double doors between the windows also have a transom, as does the window, facing Walnut Street, made from an original door. Only two of the many tall chimneys along the west wall have survived. The rhythm noticeable in the successive windows was even more evident when the building was topped with a row of repeating chimneys. Virginia Good presently owns the building.

27. Hunger Building

The corner building of three stories at Jefferson and Second streets has brick dentils and smooth lintels at the windows, characteristics which suggest construction sometime in the late 1830s, probably coincident with the erection of the second building. Both buildings received iron fronts on the first floor level possibly in the 1870s. Too, supposedly at this time, the second building was updated with an ornamental Italianate cornice.

John Pugh initially owned the corner property. In the 1850s Nicholas Lichtman held the deed. This may have been the Franklin House, which Lichtman managed in 1851. Certainly he had a coffeehouse here in 1859–60 as recorded in the city's first directory. In 1867 the building was listed as a saloon and

Robert Twente

restaurant. Five years later it was just a saloon. In 1887–88 it was the Eagle Hotel with John Jager, proprietor. In 1906 Clement Hunger bought the building from Lichtman's widow to convert it to a feed store. The structure is still in the possession of the Hunger family.

The interior of the corner building offers a good example of the use made of the upper floors of business buildings. An elaborate staircase leads from the second room on the first floor to the next level above, which served as a residence for the owner and, at times, as a hotel. A third floor ballroom, heated by a fireplace, dates from the hotel period. Still in place over the staircase is a small balcony, which the musicians utilized.

10. Madison *Daily Courier*, 2 March 1865.

Frank S. Baker

28. Pommer Building

This three-story brick house at 502 East Second Street reflects a mixture of Federal and Classic motifs. Probably a product of the early 1840s, the two-pitch roof with fractables at the gable ends corresponds to that on many Federal houses in the vicinity, but the mass and profile are strongly Classic. The fractables tie it to the row houses in the 500 block of Jefferson and to the buildings at 727–35 West Third. The east-end gable features bridged double chimneys. Three brick courses, the middle course being dentils, make up the cornice, which extends beyond the face of the wall. Windows that have not been modernized are six over six with stone sills and bricks at the top in running bond. No structural decorations are present around the entrance door on Second Street or the door on East Street.

The earliest use of the building other than as a residence is recorded in the first city directory of 1859–60. Piano dealer William Pommer used it for his business. Later in 1867 Pommer was listed as a piano manufacturer. Over a period of years a grocery operated here under various names, and at the same

time one or more families lived in the upper floors. Tradition has it that it was for a time a boardinghouse. The multiple use made of this building was common with many of the town's structures in the nineteenth century. C. Eugene and Janet McLemore are the present owners.

29. Schoenstein Building

This large cubic brick building at 501–503 Walnut, with a hip roof and standing seams, is basically Federal and was built, probably in the late 1830s, as a store and residence. The exterior facade is surmounted by brick dentils; windows have smooth stone sills and lintels. Sidelights and a large transom highlight the door to the corner shop. In the second shop from the corner the windows and door are more diminutive.

The Kampe family operated a grocery in this building from the 1860s well into the twentieth century, and a hardware store once occupied the store space to the right. The large plate-glass windows in the corner section were installed in the 1930s by Bill Bodem, who had a barber shop there. The present owners are Robert and Martha Schoenstein.

Frank S. Baker

30. Old Inn

Among the number of public houses that dotted Madison in the 1830s was this three-story brick inn at 218 Walnut Street that largely accommodated the Ohio River traveler. Richard Talbott had possession of the building at the outset. Jesse Whitehead was a later owner. Built on the line of the street, the structure has a narrow wood porch overhanging the sidewalk. The space beneath the porch was initially enclosed by a latticework set at diagonals. The standing seam roof is probably original. The current owners are Elvin and Cordelia Bell.

Frank S. Baker

31. Vawter-Coleman House

The land occupied by this house at 1534 Crozier Avenue was given to the city of North Madison by James Vawter for a school and meetinghouse. Probably built shortly after 1843, it shows many of the characteristics of Georgian architecture, such as the dormer windows, the slope of the roof, and the short windows on the first floor. In the interior there is a baseboard but no cornice, a chair rail, and a twisting staircase rising in one corner of the living room. A fireplace at the east end of the building has disappeared; a double fireplace serving the living room and a room to the west rises in the wall dividing those two rooms. The long window may have been originally a door. Attic floorboards are very wide. The entire building is crude in its construction, giving credence to the idea that it was built by volunteers. The present owners are Perry and Virginia Coleman.

Frank S. Baker

IV

Classic Revival

IT WAS THOMAS JEFFERSON who first introduced the Classic Revival style to this country. While ambassador to France he had visited the little town of Nimes and had become fascinated by the Roman ruins he found there, and most especially by the Maison Carree built in the first century B.C. This fascination, coupled with his study of the works of Palladio, inspired him to design the state capitol in Richmond, Virginia, in 1789, the first pure classical temple form in America.

However, Benjamin Henry Latrobe, who came from England in 1796, brought the style that swept the country, the Greek Revival. Two years after his arrival he designed the new bank of Pennsylvania, the first building in this country in the Classic Greek order.[1] Although the Roman style predated that of the Greek on the eastern seaboard, in Madison the Greek Revival came first and predominated. Aesthetically, practically, and philosophically, the Greek Revival was readily adaptable to the life-styles of the people in this part of the country.

Early in the nineteenth century the imagination of the American people was quickened by classical antiquity. Ancient Athens was the fount of liberty. The Greek *polis* was the ideal form of government. When members of the Indiana legislature met in Corydon in January, 1821, to name the place they had chosen for the new state capital, Jeremiah Sullivan proposed the name that combined American and Greek derivations, *Indianapolis*. In addition to the feeling that they were the spiritual successors of ancient Greece, the American people, having recently fought their own war for independence, felt great sympathy for the modern Greek nation in its struggle for political freedom. These feelings of kinship with ancient and modern Greece gave impetus to the development of Greek Revival architecture in America.

In Madison building materials were the same as in preceding periods. Brick was favored, except for dressed limestone lintels over doors and windows, and stucco was frequently applied over brick surfaces and rough stone. Stylistically, roofs were flatter, nearly disappearing, and chimneys were reduced. Ceilings were higher and windows were larger and taller than they had previously been. Shutters, inside and outside, for the most part remained. Porticos, heavy columns, pilasters, pediments, and cornices appeared. The capped pilaster was as familiar a feature as the column itself. Structures were frequently cube-like, with pilasters at the four corners and with wide Greek entablatures around the four sides of the building. This entablature might be surmounted by a hip roof, or the building might have a two-pitch roof with gable ends. In the interiors woodwork was heavily scaled. Windows and door lintels were often pedimented and sometimes or-

---

1. John Poppeliers, S. Allen Chambers, and Nancy B. Schwartz, *What Style Is It?* (Washington: The Preservation Press of the National Trust for Historic Preservation, 1977), 15.

namented with the anthemion or other Greek detail.

The Greek Revival appealed to Madisonians, not only for its aesthetic values, but because its basic structure had proportion and simplicity that could be used as a design for a small residence or a large public building. The decorative features could be added or subtracted to fit the function of the building being constructed, whether it be a home for a family of modest means or a public building such as a church or courthouse.

32. Historic Madison, Inc., Auditorium

Robert Twente

A spectacular example of Greek temple plan architecture, and the first Greek classic work in Madison, is this building at 101 East Third Street designed by Edwin J. Peck for the Second Presbyterian Church. After passing through the ownership of several different parties, the building is now owned by Historic Madison, Inc. On the northeast corner of Third and West streets, facing Third, the front facade has a recessed entrance in the distyle-in-antis mode. Above the entrance an entablature bearing Greek triglyphs rises to a fine Classic cornice. The

structure is crowned by a gable end that is enriched with a cornice simpler than the one below. The triangular area enclosed by the gable end, called a tympanum, contains no additional decoration. The exterior walls are covered with stucco, and troweled smooth. The two massive columns in the entrance, which are slightly tapered and heavily fluted, are Doric and have no special bases. The recessed entrance is flanked on either side by three matched pilasters extending to the entablature, giving a well-regulated rhythm to the entire front facade. The eaves of the two-pitched roof carry a gutter for water but are plain and display no ornamentation.

The auditorium, comprising almost all of the main floor, rests on a high foundation and is approached by eleven steps at the street entrance. This plan allows two rooms on the lower level, one behind the other, to serve as lecture halls. One of the rooms,

Interior, c. 1883   HMI

built in a pit form, later removed, resulted in a seating arrangement in ascending rows. The main auditorium has very tall windows (11 x 17⅛ inches), twelve over twelve, with clear glass. Three of these windows were placed on the west wall and three on the east wall. They had inside shutters, since lost, which folded back out of sight into casings. Windows on the lower floor had heavy outside shutters. Two small rooms flank the recessed entrance. The room to the west originally contained the 1867 Johnson tracker organ, opus 217. This handsome pipe organ, long since removed from the front of the auditorium, was restored and rededicated in 1985. The room to the east is a coatroom and contains the stairs to the lower portion of the building. Each of the anterooms has its own small window and door opening onto the recessed entrance. The lectern end of the room opposite the entrance has an extended bay which now contains the organ. Originally this room had a ceiling in the form of a plastered barrel vault, coffered with extruded plaster rosettes in the center of each coffer. It was reputed to be the finest plaster ceiling in the Northwest Territory at the time. It was razed when it began to crack. Beneath the ceiling the walls were topped by a cornice, now largely destroyed except for a small portion that survives in the two small rooms flanking the entrance. This fragment will serve as a guide when the time comes to replace the cornice that has been destroyed. The picture showing the coffered ceiling as it was in the early 1880s would likewise assist in replacing the ceiling. Two of the original benches with their very straight backs and very flat seats are now in the downstairs office of Historic Madison, Inc.

33. Lanier-Jeffery House

According to tradition a man from Pittsburgh came to Madison and deposited with the Madison bank an extremely heavy footlocker on which the bank gave him credit to start building a house at the corner of

Ward's Studio

Second and Elm streets. Before the house was finished, around 1838, he left town, leaving a large number of unpaid bills. The builders asked the bank for payment. James F. D. Lanier attempted to locate the owner in Pittsburgh and, failing to do so, paid the bills, took possession, finished the house, and for a time lived in it while his big house facing the river two blocks away was being built. Lanier used the southwest room as his personal office before his big house was finished.

Classic in style, more Roman than Greek, and cubic in form, with a two-story tetrastyle portico facing the river, this house at 302 East Elm Street has a deep cornice around the top and a pediment enclosing a three-part window surmounting the portico. Floor-length windows give access to the portico, which originally had a wood floor. The fluted columns have Doric capitals and rest on cubic bases which, according to the present owner, Mrs. Jane Jeffery, were added at a later date. A Flora photograph shows shutters on all windows and closed shutters over the entrance in the middle of the facade under the portico, hiding the fact that it was not a functional entrance. The house wall in the portico is made up of boards, tongue and grooved, to present a smooth surface imitating stone. The sides of the house have walls of weatherboarding of three different widths. The narrowest is at the bottom and below the lower window sills. Wider weatherboarding extends above this to the sills of the upper windows, and still wider boarding stretches above this to the cornice.

In *Old American Houses, 1700–1850* Henry and Ottalie Williams write regarding this graduation of width:

> *From about 1740 on, there was a vogue in some areas for graduating the exposure of the clapboards. The depth of each clapboard exposed to view gradually increased from the bottom row up, usually reaching maximum exposure somewhere near the tops of the first-floor windows. In some instances the width of the individual clapboards varies so that the overlap remains constant; in other cases the boards are all the same width and the lap varies. This variation raises a question as to whether the idea was to provide extra protection where it was most needed or was simply a decorative feature.*[2]

The house rests on a high stone foundation which has a doorway at the basement level under the portico facing Second Street. Originally the building extended much farther to the rear (north) of the lot, but service areas, which included servants' quarters, laundry, kitchens, toilets, and woodsheds, have been demolished.

Francis Costigan, Architect

Of the architects who worked in Madison, the man who unquestionably had the greatest impact on the architecture of the city was Francis Costigan. He was born in Washington, D.C., in 1810, but soon after his family moved to Baltimore, where at an early age he was engaged as a carpenter's assistant. He quickly became a skilled draftsman, and in 1835 the Baltimore directory listed him as carpenter-builder, with shops on Frederick Street. The financial depression of the late 1830s affected the building trade on the East Coast, and Costigan decided to go West. In 1836, at the age of twenty-six, he arrived in Madison to enter upon a successful career as a builder and architect in the Classic tradition. In 1851 he moved to Indianapolis where he adapted his style to fit the Gothic mode.

2. Henry Lionel Williams and Ottalie K. Williams, *Old American Houses, 1700–1850: How to Restore, Remodel, and Reproduce Them* (New York: Coward-McCann, 1957), 108. Illustrations can be seen in Nancy Sirkis, *Reflections of 1776: The Colonies Revisited* (New York: Viking, 1974), 38–39, and G. E. Kidder Smith, *A Pictorial History of Architecture in America*, 2 vols. (New York: American Heritage, 1976), 1:46–47, 58–59, 71.

Ward's Studio

34. Holstein-Whitsitt House

This house at 718 West Main Street may well be the first structure built by Francis Costigan after his arrival in Madison in 1836. In style it closely resembles the New England houses in Portsmouth and Salem of this or a slightly earlier period: cubical, with a prominent hip roof, widow's walk with balustrade, recessed doorway, and brick pilasters at the corners. The windows are double hung, and those on the first floor are six over six and stop two feet from the floor. The original muntins were later cut out of the windows facing the street to make place for the single panes. Rear porches were glassed around 1901. Cherry and maple flooring was also added about the same time, as were closets in the bedrooms, flanking the fireplaces and under the stairs. A balustrade surmounting the house encircled a flat deck that was reached by a staircase from the second floor. The service wing at the rear with gabled roof and full basement appears to be contemporary with the main portion of the house.

Jacob Shuh, an industrialist, held the property originally. Subsequent owners included Louis Holstein and Dr. S. A. Whitsitt. The present owners are Ronald and Evangeline Greves.

35. Lanier Memorial

This house at 511 West First Street, designed and built by architect-builder Francis Costigan for Madison's famous banker, James F. D. Lanier, is now nationally known. It was constructed during the years 1840–44, and its design came from various sources, particularly Minard Lafever's carpenters' handbooks. Costigan was strongly influenced by the great Baltimore houses which he had studied before coming to Madison. It was, however, his deep sense of proportion, coupled with his own fertile imagination, that distinguished his work and differentiated it from that of his contemporaries.

Classic, cubic, and massive, the Lanier house is not quite a temple form. It has no pediment, and the roof is not visible from the ground level. Instead, a slightly pedimented fascia board or shield board, which goes around all four sides and is decorated by a molding similar to those that appear around the windows, hides the roof. Anthemion carvings occur at the centers and at the corners of the four sides. A massive cupola that is reminiscent of a Greek choragic monument or the Tower of the Winds in Athens rises some sixteen feet above the stairwell in the center of the house and crowns the building. The whole gives an impression of grandeur hitherto unknown in this river town.

A number of architectural features serve to increase this feeling of splendor. The first is the great height of the columns on the river facade. These reach from the high basement above the ground level to the cornice two and a half floors above. The wing at the side of the house, which rises one full story from the ground on a high foundation and is topped by a second story behind a mansard roof, was added somewhat later.

A double divided staircase on the terrace facing the river at the garden entrance added to the estate-like effect, as did the two greenhouses, which supplied both flowers and fruit for the Laniers. The foundation of one of these can still be seen in the garden near the house. This effect was heightened at a later date by a wall between the garden and the river and the rather high iron fence with gates on the three sides of the garden.

The street facade must have seemed equally imposing to guests arriving by carriage. The house was built only a few feet back from the street at a time when First Street continued through the block. That street was not closed until a few years ago when the park between First and Second streets was created. Guests arriving by carriage would alight on the sidewalk and be completely overwhelmed by this vast masonry facade looming above them. Much of that effect was lost when the street was closed.

On the south face of the house toward the river the windows on the first level are tall and narrow, being six over nine. On the second level they are six over six, with a triple window above the entrance. On the third level round windows ornamented with wreaths of carved leaves pierce the frieze. On the sides of the house windows are all six over six, but those on the first floor are two feet longer than those above. This arrangement exemplifies Costigan's sensitivity to space relations. The windows on the street side duplicate those on the river side. Window caps are further decorated with carved rosettes. There are no exterior shutters but only wide Classic window framing. Ironwork decorating the house is heavy and elaborate and includes a railing around the

HABS/HAER

portico, down the steps, and around the balconies at the street windows on the first floor.

The porch at the entrance on the street side has capitals on the columns that do not match those on the river side, for which reason it has been suggested that this porch was a later addition. Early photographs show that the mansard roof was added at a later date, and that the ceiling of the second floor in the wing was raised at the time the mansard roof was constructed, probably in the early 1870s. A lithograph from 1876 shows the bay window and the roof, proving their existence by that date. A photograph

Carriage entrance   *HABS/HAER*

Column capital   *HABS/HAER*

Staircase   *HABS/HAER*

Anthemion acroterion on cornice   *HABS/HAER*

dating from the 1860s shows the service wing as a one-story structure.[3]

The central hall contains a cantilevered spiral staircase, recessed into a side wall, making a full turn between floors. The hall is flanked by a double parlor on one side and by a dining room, stairs, and a library on the other. A small transverse hall between the dining room and the library leads to the service wing.

The double parlor is divided by sliding doors flanked by columns with Ionic capitals. These parlors are ornamented with cornices and heavy window casings. The cornices are plaster and decorated with egg-and-dart moldings and dentils. Windows on the east and west walls have panels beneath them extending to the floor, making them compatible with the floor-length windows on the other sides. Upper and lower inside shutters on these windows provide excellent heat control in the summer and winter. These shutters are solid panels and fold back into the window framing when not in use. At an early period south windows had awnings. These were not the large Victorian awnings covering half of a window but rather were small multiple awnings, one above another and at least three or four on a window.

Fireplaces heated the double parlors, dining room, library, and the bedrooms on the second floor. On the first floor the mantels are black Italian marble, and on the second they are black in the two south bedrooms and almost white in the two north ones. The fireplaces in the bedrooms have been altered since the building has been owned by the state. The third floor rooms were heated by stoves.

Door and window casings on the second floor are decorated with ogee or cyma recta moldings, centered on a raised V-shape member, and surmounted by bulls' eyes at the corners. Dressing rooms between the bedrooms on the second floor occupied nearly five feet, and a water closet was added to one of them in the 1870s. The water for it had to be pumped daily from a cistern.

In the transverse hall at the foot of the curved stairs Costigan placed one of his now famous curved doors, which opens into the service hall. Another curved door opens from the stairwell to the third floor hall.

Vents in the cupola represent Costigan's early efforts at heat control and ventilation. They can be opened or closed and thus can control the movement of warm air from the house. Costigan's School for the Blind in Indianapolis better demonstrated such controls. See also the discussion of the Shrewsbury house.

Drusilla Cravens, granddaughter of James F. D. Lanier, later owned the house. In 1925 the State of Indiana acquired the residence and opened it in 1926 as the state's first historical memorial. The Indiana Department of Conservation is its present owner.

---

3. Photograph by J. R. Gorgas, now in the Indiana State Library.

Robert Twente

36. Costigan Double House

This fine example of Classic Greek design in brick and stone was built at 415–17 Vine Street about 1840 and may have been Francis Costigan's third architectural venture in Madison. Costigan built this double house and resided in the south end and rented the north end. Fine cornice and caps over the entrance doors have dentils that are shaped like tapered spools, quite like the guttae found in ancient Greek works. Twin recessed doorways have pilasters on the outer entrance, paneled reveals, and narrow sidelights flanking the inner doors. Twin chimneys at either end of the house rise from unbroken end walls. The stone foundation is prominent. Dressed stone blocks are laid with raked mortar joints and surmounted by a stone band that encircles the house.

The houses are now owned by Edward and Jean Cooper (415) and Angeline Ennis (417).

37. Shrewsbury House

Francis Costigan designed another of his Classic houses in Madison for Capt. Charles Lewis Shrewsbury, commission merchant, meatpacker, flour mill owner, and, in later years, mayor of the city. Built in 1846–49, the house is located at 301 West First Street, and is situated on the eastern half of a block whose western side was occupied by another house designed by Costigan. This home was built for Mrs. Shrewsbury's parents, Mr. and Mrs. John Woodburn, and it was demolished in 1928. The street sides of the house are bound by an iron fence and a herringbone brick sidewalk.

More conservative and restrained in design than the Lanier house, the style of the Shrewsbury house follows closely that of the Classic Baltimore houses. Large and cubic in form, it is built of hand-polished pink brick and surmounted by a majestic entablature and cornice that completely surround the house. The entablature is decorated with elaborate moldings and dentils. A hip roof rises to a platform, originally with a balustrade which has been removed. Designed with

W. H. Bass Photo Co.

two main entrances, the one on the north facing High Street has a recessed portal and a door twelve feet tall. The garden entrance on the south side has a portico supported by fluted columns and a door also twelve feet tall. Both doorways have sidelights. The service wing is placed on the west side of the house, away from Poplar Street.

The house shows evidence that Costigan made great use of the carpenters' handbooks being published during the first half of the nineteenth century, notably the works of Asher Benjamin and Minard Lafever. The design for the iron fence was taken from the handbook of Asher Benjamin. The iron balconies which flank both the street and garden entrances have the pattern of the palmetto and the anthemion or honeysuckle, also taken from Benjamin's designs.[4] It is quite possible that Costigan, with wry humor, chose the palmetto to suggest that the funds to pay for the house came from the captain's Palmetto Mills.

The design for the recessed entrance on the street side can be found in Lafever's *Beauties of Modern Architecture*. The designs for the cornice and entablature at the crown of the house can also be found in Lafever. And yet, Costigan was more apt to adapt than to copy. A striking example of his ingenuity in fitting an old pattern to his own use is seen in the columns supporting the garden portico, where the capitals are derived from the bud of the Egyptian lotus. Since Lafever seems never to have created a capital from the bud of the blossom, Costigan may have designed that bud capital himself.

Exterior window lintels and door lintels are slightly pedimented in smooth stone and are decorated with an acroterion at the peak in the form of the anthemion and again at the extreme corner angles

with a half-anthemion. Panes in the windows measure 12¾ inches by 25⅝ inches.

In the interior of the Shrewsbury house, the spiral staircase is undoubtedly Costigan's most spectacular achievement. The original design came from Lafever's *The Modern Practice of Staircase and Handrail Construction*. The staircase rises from the center of the front hall to the top of the house and is freestanding and self-supporting. The weight is concentrated on the bottom step and is carried by the end of the steps and the curved drum which is made up of four layers of laminated wood, each about a quarter of an inch thick. The steps are pine, painted white to resemble marble, and the railing is cherry. Where the curved railing becomes tangent to the wall, there is a saucer or depression in the plaster that follows the curve of the handrail so that knuckles do not hit the wall. Today, as then, the staircase serves as the air conditioner for the house — the hot air rising to the top and escaping out the attic windows.

The drawing room is a double cube, partially divided by two pairs of fluted columns.[5] The capitals are modified Corinthian, and the Egyptian lotus blossom, half open, is taken from Lafever.[6] This capital was introduced into the area by Costigan in the tetrastyle portico of the Lanier house (1840–44),

4. Asher Benjamin, *The Builder's Guide, Illustrated by Sixty-six Engravings, Which Exhibit the Orders of Architecture and Other Elements of the Art: Designed for the Use of Builders and Joiners* (Boston: Perkins and Marvin; Philadelphia: Henry Perkins, 1839).

5. The first known pairs of disengaged columns without doors to partially divide a long room were made by Alexander Jackson Davis in a house designed for John C. Stevens, College Place and Murray Street, New York City. The original drawing is held by the New-York Historical Society.

6. Minard Lafever, *The Beauties of Modern Architecture*, vol. 18 of *Da Capo Press Series in Architecture and Decorative Art* (New York: Da Capo Press, 1968), plate 11.

and he repeated the design in the Shrewsbury drawing room (1846–49). The same capital was used by Matthew Temperly in the ballroom of the Washington Firehouse on West Third Street in 1848 or 1849.

The design in the drawing room shows Costigan's growth and maturity as an architect. Here the many vertical lines which occur in the columns and in the pilasters at the sides of the windows, in the corners, and opposite the columns in the side walls are integrated with the elaborate plaster cornice at the top and with the panels in the ceiling. The room becomes a single unit in its decoration. This is the first time that Costigan achieved a design in which he treated an entire room as a whole.

In the Shrewsbury house interior Costigan made use of the newest developments in dimensions and proportions. He used greater verticals, taller doors, and higher ceilings than had ever been used in domestic architecture in this country. Full-length windows have thirteen feet of glass. On the first floor, wide and heavy door and window casings taper to a dogleg which extends the lintel the width of the taper. The taper in the door casing gives the appearance of verticality, actually an optical illusion. On the second floor, door and window casings are similar but lack the projecting cap.

Another special design evident in the Shrewsbury house is the traffic pattern. The front hall extends the entire depth of the house, with the drawing room on the east side and two rooms on the west side. Beyond these two rooms is a wing with two additional rooms, each having two exits or entrances, thus allowing for a smooth traffic pattern. This same pattern is repeated on the second floor. The third floor is an attic

without walls, except for those around the perimeter and encircling the staircase.

Fireplaces are extremely well designed. One of the important design features is a simple device called a check draft. At the back of the hearth at floor level an aperture about four and a half inches square opens into a channel back into the chimney some eighteen inches and then turns at right angles and continues vertically until it opens into the main chimney at the height of the mantel shelf. When the check drafts are closed, the fire burns like a blowtorch, and the heat goes up the chimney. When the check drafts are

Garden Entrance   *HABS/HAER*

Drawing room   *HABS/HAER*

open, the fire simmers along at a good pace and takes the cold air off the floor through the channel. As the cold air is expelled from the room, the heat comes forward and can be felt on the wall at the opposite side of the room. Thirteen fireplaces supplied the heat for the house. All but those in the two kitchens burned coal. Wood was preferred for cooking because of the flavor it imparted, hickory or beech for meats, fruit wood for baking.

In addition to his use of the fireplaces, Costigan employed the principle of solar heat. The original dining room with its south window was designed so that the sunlight, even on the shortest day of the year, extends the full length of the room, giving the greatest amount of heat. All other south windows with their great height admit equal amounts of sunlight.

The Shrewsbury garden, on the south side of the house, offered a magnificent view of the Ohio River and the Kentucky hills beyond. Less formal and more intimate than that of the Lanier garden, the Shrewsbury garden nevertheless possessed an architectural design. Laid out in quadrangles with a path running down the middle, the garden resembled the first floor plan of the house, with its central hall and rooms on either side. It was used as were the rooms within. In the morning when the sun was in the east, the family and guests could sit in one area and move to more comfortable areas as the day progressed. It was a flower garden, and many of the old plants and shrubs still bloom each spring and summer. There was also space for tennis or croquet. The area below the garden, separated by a hedge and a thirty-inch concealed wall or ha-ha, was pasture land that stretched to the river. In the corner nearest the house and adjacent to Poplar Street stood the carriage house, which has long since disappeared.

Writing of the Lanier and Shrewsbury houses, Rex Newcomb paid this tribute to Francis Costigan: "These two residences, had he designed nothing else, would secure his name to posterity."[7] The present owners of the Shrewsbury house are John and Ann Windle.

7. Rexford Newcomb, *Architecture of the Old Northwest Territory: A Study of Early Architecture in Ohio, Indiana, Illinois, Michigan, Wisconsin, and Part of Minnesota* (Chicago: University of Chicago Press, 1950), 85.

38. Costigan House

HABS/HAER

Entrance   *HABS/HAER*

Drawing room and entrance   *HABS/HAER*

Francis Costigan attained not only a national reputation as an architect and master builder by building the Lanier and Shrewsbury houses, but apparently he achieved considerable economic security by the time of their completion as well. Between 1846 and 1849 he built for himself a fine home at 408 West Third Street. This home Costigan fashioned with such skill and imagination that architects of today consider it a masterpiece of design for a narrow lot. Land at this time was already expensive in Madison, and Costigan had been trained in Baltimore where narrow street frontage was traditional. Hence, he did not hesitate

Staircase   *HABS/HAER*

to build on a strip of land scarcely twenty-two feet wide, yet he constructed a house with a magnificent drawing room thirty feet long with bow end, twin fireplaces, and a fine, high ceiling with deeply depressed panels, heavily ornamented with egg-and-dart moldings gilded in the Greek manner. The columns of the portico are Greek inspired without bases, the flutes going straight to the stone base. The columns have modified Corinthian capitals that are dominated by a design drawn from the Egyptian lotus blossom when it is partly opened but not yet curled. This central blossom is ringed by a circle of small acanthus leaves. The entablature over the entrance repeats the main entablature. The ceiling of the portico is deeply coffered and heavily decorated. The house also shows Costigan's characteristically fine woodwork, including both curved and sliding doors and an interesting stepladder staircase with a now famous push gate at the top. Thelma Schoenstein now owns the property.

39. Steinhardt House

The house at 1120 Michigan Road has a hipped roof characteristic of the Classic style. Interrupted by gables facing four ways, the slate roof has a flat platform or deck in its center. Windows are floor length in the Classic manner. The six fluted columns of the porch have Ionic capitals. A raised central portion of the porch roof gives the impression that originally there was a portico and that the porch was extended the full length of the front of the house at a later date. A pressed-metal ceiling covers the porch and has a pressed-metal cove where it attaches to the house. In the main block of the house four chimneys, two at each end, service four fireplaces, one in the outer wall of each of the four main rooms of the house.

Robert Twente

Woodwork is fluted and deeply carved around doors and windows. The double drawing room has fluted columns in the middle serving as dividers. The leaves and blossoms in the capitals are similar to those at the entrance of the Costigan house on Third Street. This similarity lends credence to the belief that Costigan was involved in the design of the

Robert Twente

Steinhardt house.[8] However, the deeply carved decorations do not occur in any house known to have been designed by Costigan, so they should not be considered characteristic of his work. Seams in the walls and ceiling in no way represent Costigan's fine craftsmanship.

The design of the columns and their similarity to those in the Costigan house on Third Street furnish a basis for the belief that at least a portion of the house was built at about the same time as the Costigan house, that is, 1846–49. There is a tradition, however, that this building, or a portion of it, was the house lived in by the keeper of the tollgate at this point on the Michigan Road much earlier than the late 1840s. Paul and Dorothy Steinhardt now own the house.

follow the Classic tradition. The bargeboard undoubtedly was a later addition. Other alterations at the rear and on the interior have been extensive and obviously recent. Among the later owners of the house was John Wesbecker. George and Patricia Alcorn now own the property.

40. Marsh-Wesbecker House

The John Marsh house, high upon Telegraph Hill to the east of Madison, is another residence that has been linked to Costigan, although no proof to this effect has been found. Telegraph Hill derived its name during the Civil War when a telegraph station was placed on the lofty vantage point. When Marsh built his house on the brow of the hill in 1851, it was called Mount Marsh. The ground plan of the residence, a block with wings, the whole forming the shape of a capital letter S, provided three magnificent panoramic views of the river and town. The wings have since been removed. At the time of construction a Madison paper described it as "an elegant summer cottage of the Swiss, Tuscan or Gothic style."[9] The iron balconies with their lyre design and the Ionic columns on the portico, along with the brick dentils,

41. Dr. Hutchings Office

This building at 120 West Third Street contains two rooms on the first floor, two on the second, and a basement. Before Dr. Hutchings acquired the building it had been the law office of Michael G. Bright and later Judge John Cravens. Built at some point between 1838 and 1848, it is a good example of the Greek Revival style, with a fine, small pediment on the street side and simple moldings and cornice board. Brick dentils on the sides are also characteristic of the Classical Greek Revival. The foundation is of cut stone.

8. The capitals on the columns in the drawing rooms are identified as an "early form of Greek Corinthian capital" in Cyril M. Harris, ed., *Dictionary of Architecture and Construction* (New York: McGraw-Hill, 1975), 138.
9. Madison *Daily Courier*, 18 April 1851.

Surgery   *HABS/HAER*

The two rooms on the first floor were the reception room and a surgery. The two bedrooms on the second floor comprised one of the earliest facilities in the valley until the present hospital in Madison was started in 1899. Stenciling occurs at the top of walls in the surgery and includes figures, some seated and some standing. These figures are located at intervals, with the spaces between filled with geometric patterns. The geometric patterns, all in black, cover the ceiling. Other buildings in town in which stenciling has been found are the Francisco-Jordan house, the Levy-Swarts house, the "Eggleston" house, and the old Firehouse No. 4 on Walnut Street. Early wiring for lights was placed across the ceilings in wood moldings which had two deep grooves, one for each wire. Samples of these have been preserved. The latches on the shutters and window sills allowed the shutters to be fastened in several different positions. The iron grills on the windows are recent.

After Dr. Hutchings died in 1903, the contents of his office were carefully labeled and packed away by his daughters. His belongings have been since returned to their original places in the office, which was opened as the Hutchings Museum in 1973. The property was presented in 1969 to Historic Madison, Inc., by a granddaughter of Dr. Hutchings, Mrs. Elisabeth Zulauf Kelemen.

HABS/HAER

42. White-Koehler House

HMI

The Classic brick building located at 318 Broadway, adjacent to the Koehler building, is on a lot purchased by Alexander White, a carpenter and builder, in 1872 for $8,167. This price indicates that the building was probably built in the 1850s and already on the site. Born in Scotland in 1821, White came to Madison in 1849 from Virginia. He built a number of business houses and private residences in Madison, and he served a term, 1874–76, as the city's first Republican mayor. White died in Madison in 1883.

One room deep and two stories high, the house has a Classic cornice with dentils and windows facing the street and the rear. The original windows are six over six. Lintels are stone, flush, and flat, without ornament. Wood pilasters, which are lacking their original bases, and a projecting cornice frame a somewhat recessed doorway. A deeply paneled door with narrow sidelights is in the recess. The stone steps and their end supports show red strata similar to those in the stone that came from the second railroad cut. The roof is standing seam and is probably original. A porch at the back under the main body of the house has been removed. On the whole, the building displays fine and easy proportions, comfortable mass, and rhythmic symmetry. Frederick and Judith Koehler are the present owners.

Frank S. Baker

43. Cowden-Dunlap House

This house at 111 West Third Street displays characteristics of the Classic mode: unornamented cornice and frieze board and smooth flat lintels above the windows and door. The window sashes are divided into six panes over six. The roof is not visible from the street. The house was built by John Cowden between 1845 and 1847. When the kitchen fireplace was reopened in a recent restoration, the original crane and hook were found in place. The present owner is Brenda Dunlap.

44. Witt-Demaree House

The early records of the lot at 111 West Second Street are confused and give no information from 1826 to 1853. However, the records do indicate the existence of some sort of building at the early date and a more substantial building at the later date. Originally the house contained a double parlor on the first floor, a staircase that went to the third floor, and a basement kitchen with cooking fireplace and brick floor under the rear parlor. The kitchen had a wide outside entrance. The two rooms at the rear of the original house were of a much later date.

At one time this house was the residence of the superintendent of the Madison Woolen Mills, established in 1870, which adjoined it on the east. The Woolen Mills owned part of the land between this house and the Luke Apartments on the corner to the west. Poetess Sarah Bolton once lived in this house. Benning Witt held title to the property at an early date. William and Betty Demaree now own the real estate.

Frank S. Baker

45. Schussler House

This house at 514 Jefferson Street has a Classic facade with slightly pedimented stone lintels above the windows and a cornice made up of dentils and beaded moldings which does not extend to the corners of the building. A smaller, similar cornice decorates the recessed entrance. Iron railings at the steps show the lyre as a decorative element. The steps are cut stone, possibly from Portsmouth, Ohio. An areaway at the front, enclosed by an iron fence with a double gate, at one time held a staircase leading to a door into the basement under the entrance.

Charles Schussler purchased the lot in 1849, a fact suggesting that the house was built then or in the early 1850s. In the directories for 1859 and later years, Dr. Schussler was listed as residing and practicing medicine at this address. The basement rooms with their separate entrance on the street were probably used as his office. This is an example of architecture that was modified to accommodate different uses of the same structure, in this instance a doctor's office in a residence. William Detmer presently owns the structure.

Robert Twente

HABS/HAER

46. Dillon-Ross House

This house at 212 East Street is another example of a brick block at the line of the sidewalk on a cut foundation. It is capped by a cornice which is entablature-like, containing moldings and dentils, and which does not quite reach the corners. Windows are six over six. The recessed door has sidelights and a square transom. The entrance is enclosed by an iron railing ornamented with the lyre. This rail descends with the steps to street level, where it terminates in a scroll which follows the curve of the step, sometimes called a curtail step. The similarities between this house and the one at 514 Jefferson Street indicate a probable construction date of the early 1850s. The plat was registered in 1846. Service portions of the building, which extend along the alley, include two brick structures which were probably a carriage house and stables. Originally owned by Patrick Dillon, a boot and shoe dealer, the house later was held by John Ross. Today it is the property of the Jefferson County Youth Shelter.

47. Green-Grayson House

This house at 624 East Second Street might have been built as late as 1853. If so, the appearance of brick dentils in the cornice would be indicative of their use over a prolonged period as a decorative motif. Indeed brick dentils are found in buildings south of the courthouse that were seemingly constructed between 1835 and 1839. This house at Second and Baltimore streets, however, is located at a considerable distance from the old center of town, a fact which might account for the appearance of this decorative motif at such a late date. The unornamented lintels over the windows and the plain cornice are more characteristic of a pre-classical style, and the side galleries, with solid round posts that have disk-like caps and a balustrade with square balusters, are clearly reminiscent of work of the Federal period. Furthermore, the porch ceilings are

German Collection

made up of planks six to eight inches wide and with a single bead on one side only. These planks are laid crosswise on the lower porch and lengthwise on the upper porch. A similar ceiling is found on the lower side gallery of the Talbott-Hyatt house built prior to 1820.

The carriage house behind the Green-Grayson residence is a brick building with gable end facing the street that contains large double doors with strap hinges of wrought iron and a hay door in the gable above. On the south face of the building there is a door with stone lintel and two windows, one on the ground floor level and one on the hayloft level, each with six panes. On the west face a double-hung window has six over six panes. A door with a stone lintel, slightly pedimented, faces the garden on the north side of the building. This doorway is flanked by stone blocks in the base of the brick wall. Another door at the west end of this face may have been cut in

at a later date. There are two iron rings set into the bricks for the hitching horses, one on the east wall and one on the south wall on the alley. Early owners of the property included George Green and George Grayson. John McGuire and Mary Goldsmith are the present owners.

48. "Helm" House

This house at 610 West Main Street is simple Classic in style with caps on the windows similar to those on the Costigan house on Third Street. It has long windows on the first floor front, nine over nine, that once opened onto an iron balcony, since destroyed. Windows on the second floor are six over six, and a simple Classic cornice displays dentils. On the west wall wood pilasters flank a slightly recessed doorway

Carriage house   *German Collection*

Frank S. Baker

and support a cornice with dentils. Three chimneys rise from the west wall. The roof is invisible from the street.

John Vawter bought the property from David White in 1856 and sold it in March, 1864, to Peter Weber, owner of the Union Brewery, established in 1863, which adjoined to the east. During the Civil War this house was the home of Mrs. Emilie Todd Helm, a half-sister of Mrs. Abraham Lincoln. Her husband, Gen. Ben Hardin Helm, was a Confederate officer who was killed at Chickamauga. The widow left her home in Lexington, Kentucky, on account of hostile war feelings at the time. After she came to Madison she played the organ in the Episcopal Church. Marion and Virginia Hall are the present owners.

Robert Twente

49. Frevert-Schnaitter House

This long rectangular brick building at 740 West Main Street has the simplicity of design characteristic of the early Classic style. Built probably in the 1850s, its early owners included August Frevert and the McLelland family. Windows are six over six on first and second levels and do not go to the floor. Until recently they had the original heavy shutters with movable louvers. The wooden cornice is very shallow and decorated with dentils. Dentils recur on the cornice of the portico. The front entrance has a tall door with equally tall, narrow sidelights. According to the late Judge Paul Schnaitter, the portico was added at a later date and came from the cargo of a boat from the South which was in Northern waters when the Civil War broke out. The boat unloaded its cargo in Madison in order to move more quickly downstream, and this portico along with the other cargo was sold at auction. The iron fence surrounding the house was made probably in Madison in 1865 for the courthouse lawn in Versailles, Indiana, and recently moved to its present location. Spencer and Laura Schnaitter now own the house.

Frank S. Baker

50. Yater House

The smooth, undecorated window sills and the lintels above the windows and doors, together with the brick dentils, place this structure at 119 West Third Street among the buildings of the Classic period. The date of its construction is probably the 1840s. The windows on the street facade have heavy exterior shutters, and the lower windows have interior shutters. Gables face east, west, and south. Upper and lower side galleries are at the rear on the east side. Herman Yater presently holds the property.

51. West Second Street Classic

Frank S. Baker

Probably built in the late 1840s, this brick building at 803 West Second Street is basically Classic. All windows are six over six, but panes in the windows on the lower level are long enough to reach the floor. The size of these panes suggests an installation date in the late 1840s. The lintels are stone, flush, and smooth, and the cornice with moldings gives the semblance of an entablature and is strongly reminiscent of the Classic influence, as is the lack of overhang at the gable end. The owners at present are Phillip and Cheryl Cooper.

52. Stapp-Bach House

Frank S. Baker

The oldest parts of this house at 732 West Main Street, those at the rear and at the west end, were built probably between 1828 and 1832. The east portion most likely went up in the 1840s. Wings at the back have been successively built and later destroyed. When Bach bought the house in 1906, he tore down twelve rooms, leaving it in its present state. There is internal evidence on the front of a portico or other massive structure, long since destroyed. Windows to the floor on the first level of the front facade have been blocked up to a distance of two feet from the floor. The balustrade on the roof is a replacement on the lines of the original. The pictured porch is more recent.

A very interesting staircase in the front hall leads to rooms on the second floor and to the platform on the roof. A long dining room could accommodate large groups or it could be reduced in size by lowering a swinging partition from the ceiling.

Milton Stapp (1792–1869) was born in Kentucky and came to Madison in 1816. He served in the state legislature and held the office of Lieutenant Governor, 1828–31. A lawyer by profession, he was also a merchant, bank cashier, and editor of the Madison *Daily Banner*. He was Madison's mayor in the boom years from 1850 to 1853. Stapp owned the house when Henry Clay spoke from the lawn on October 8, 1844. Subsequent owners included Albert Bach and Lloyd Jones. The present owners are William and Ann Jenner.

53. Rea House

Constructed between 1845 and 1849, this house at 427 East Main Street is built directly on the sidewalk and includes Classic features such as a cornice with

Frank S. Baker

brick dentils, slightly pedimented lintels above the windows, and six panes over six. The door casing at the entrance is tapered and shows a dogleg at the top and an extended cap with dentils. The iron railing at the entrance is recent, but the fence with its star and circle gate dates from the nineteenth century. Joseph Rea, who operated a livery stable, initially held the property. Emmett Wood later owned it. Ted Todd, Michael Walro, and Lonnie Collins now own it.

54. Pindell-Vail House

The Classic influence is strongly felt in this 1840s house at 516 West Street, with its entablature on the street facade, smooth stone lintels over the windows,

Robert Twente

low-pitched roof, simple, slightly projecting eaves, and general mass and profile. The windows are two over two. Shutters with movable louvers are probably original. The slightly recessed doorway with its fine elliptical transom was added by Dana Vail. An ell toward the back has side galleries that were popular

in Madison at the time. The side entrance in the gable end, facing the garden instead of the street, is reminiscent of a mode found in Charleston, South Carolina. Richard Pindell, a furniture dealer and builder, first owned the real estate. The First Presbyterian Church held it later as did Dana Vail. Wilma Vail is the present owner.

55. Francisco-Bramwell House

According to Carter Bramwell, the present owner, this house on Highway 7 at Paper Mill Road was built in 1861 by the Francisco family. The bricks were made on the site, and remnants of the old kilns still exist. The house has been in Bramwell's family for three generations. The porch was added in 1906. The bakehouse-smokehouse building at the side of the main house has been used as a model in designing the one reconstructed at the rear of the Jeremiah Sullivan house in Madison. It is the best surviving example of such a building among the several that were originally in the area, including the one behind Breitenbach's Grocery on Walnut Street and the one behind another Francisco building at Wirt.

Frank S. Baker

The house is brick with a cornice of wood, heavy and denticulated around the front portion of the house and lighter with moldings around the rear. The gable end is deeply pedimented with dentils. There are three areas with slightly arched openings for carriages toward the south. Wood for the fireplaces was stored in this carriage area.

56. Pitcher House

The Pitcher house at 708 East Main Street is an example of two definite and very different styles. The street facade is Classic, while the rear is strongly Italianate. Abijah Pitcher, a dry goods and pork merchant and an insurance agent, bought the property in 1839, and it remained in the possession of members of the Pitcher family until 1932. The initial construction was probably done in the 1840s.

The cornice at the eaves is deep and composed of a wide board topped by a strongly delineated molding of dentils and bead and reel design. The entrance has a recessed doorway with sidelights and cornice similar but simpler than the one at the eaves. Double-hung sash windows on the first level are six over nine and extend to the floor. The second story windows are six over six. Lintels are slightly pedimented. The house extends very deep on the lot, and the exterior wall on the east or alley side is continuous from the front past the formal rooms and thereafter past a second two-and-a-half-story section which has a camelback roof with eaves on the west side. The east wall then continues past a lower camelback section also having gutters on the west side, and finally past a carriage house under a camelback roof draining to the east with a carriage door facing the south.

Robert Twente

Italianate alterations have occurred in the back of the house but always on the west side facing the garden. This section includes a two-story bay and upper and lower side galleries, with wood lace decoration. A lead-lined water tank in the attic was the basis of one of the early water systems in the town. The house is guarded by a highly ornamented iron fence. Roger and Diane Terry own the house at present.

57. Wilson House

The distinguished doorway of this building at 315 East Second Street is an example of the Classic style, with semi-engaged columns surmounted by a half-circle window framed in moldings and half-circle of stone. Two stone steps lead to the door. An iron boot scraper is mounted on the lower step. The door itself is a replacement.

Descendants of David Wilson, the builder, came to Madison with information which enabled them to identify the house by its doorway. Wilson came at the age of fourteen from Ireland to Philadelphia, where he attended a private school, learned the craft of wood carving, and became a cabinetmaker. In 1818 he married in Lexington, Kentucky, and moved soon thereafter to Madison where he worked as a furniture maker for the rest of his life.[10]

In a Madison newspaper of 1867 Wilson's house, put up for sale, is described as comprising nine rooms, cellar, hall, and cistern, along with a stable, carriage house, and wood house.[11] Basically Classic, the house may have been built as early as 1823. Though retaining its smooth window caps and a wood cornice showing a few horizontal lines, the house was extensively refurbished towards the end of the century. At that time all windows but one were changed from six over six to one over one; a stair window was given stained glass panes; and porches were updated. A rear door has a lintel of wedged bricks. Some rear windows show no lintels; instead, bricks are laid directly across the wood frame. The cornice on the front stops short of the corner, as is the case on the house at 514 Jefferson and the one at 212 East Street and others. The present owner is the Jefferson County Health Department.

Entrance   *Frank S. Baker*

58. Cogley House

Alexander White built this house in 1851 for Thomas Cogley. Located at 509 West Main Street, the house is Classic with Italianate additions. It displays a heavy Italianate cornice that extends deep on the wall and is supported by brackets. The windows have shutters and slightly pedimented lintels on the street facade. The lintels on the alley side are flush and unornamented, showing the influence of an earlier stylistic period. The entrance doorway is recessed with sidelights. Glass in the front door is leaded and divided into small diamond panes. Panels occur in the reveals and the ceiling of the recess. The cornice over the entrance projects slightly and is supported by consoles. A row of small dentils surmounted by a row of modillions ornaments the cornice of the doorway. Iron balconies appear at two of the upper windows on the front. The roof has

10. "The Editor's Attic: David Wilson-Midwestern Cabinet Maker," *Antiques* 48(October, 1945): 319. See also Betty Lawson Walters, *Furniture Makers of Indiana, 1793 to 1850* (Indianapolis: Indiana Historical Society *Publications*, vol. 25, no. 1, 1972), 223.
11. Madison *Daily Courier*, 14 September 1867.

gables facing the east and west, and at the rear of the house there is a camelback with eaves on the east side. The rear portion of the house was appended in later years and had upper and lower porches on the east side. June Moriarity now holds the property.

Robert Twente

59. "Town House"

The earliest portion of this building at 416 East Second Street existed by 1837, and the remainder of the house was built in various stages toward the street. The house apparently was completed in 1860. The east half of this lot was sold by John Sanders to Neal McNaughton in 1837 for $1,000. This amount of money indicates that a building was standing at the time. In 1856, when Allen McNaughton sold the lot

Robert Twente

to Isaiah Weyer, it contained a brick house occupied by a tenant, Ezra Butler. In 1858 Weyer sold the lot to William Fitch for $2,500, indicating further construction between 1837 and 1858, at which time the building was still occupied by Butler. Fitch bought the west half of the lot, along the alley, from Thomas Henson in April, 1860, for $1,160.

The house is basically Classic with a bracketed Italianate cornice that may be pressed metal. The cornice returns on the west end but not on the east, where it terminates with a large bracket. A deeply recessed Classic entrance leads to a tall door with sidelights. Windows on the street face are tall and floor length. The upper windows open onto an iron balcony decorated with three lyre designs. In these upper windows the six over nine panes were retained when the lower ones were brought up to date with one over one sash. The fence, mounted on heavy stones, has posts with pineapple finials, and the gate repeats the lyre design.

The older portions of this house extend to the alley to the south and to the alley to the west and contain service areas, stable, and carriage house. The present owners are James and Rita Boone.

60. Cummins-Olmstead House

Likely constructed in the early 1840s, this large cubic house stands at 1229 West Main Street at the entrance to the country club. It displays a hip roof and a flat deck that originally had a balustrade. Initially it had a cornice with wide entablature on all four sides, but in the course of years the west and north facades were updated by changing the cornice to the modish Italianate design with brackets and modillions. The Classic porch facing the street appears to be original. The east facade has a recessed porch on the second level displaying two Doric fluted columns. The only openings on the east are within the recessed porch. There is a modern extension on

Frank S. Baker

the first level beneath the balcony. The south facade toward the river displays the original Classic entablature and cornice. A row of dentils divides the architrave from the frieze. This south front is divided by four wide brick pilasters that project only slightly. All four pilasters are stuccoed for emphasis. The panel between the two middle pilasters contains what must have been a rather imposing doorway with panels at the sides (which may have been sidelights) and a transom. A second floor entrance directly above the first is equally recessed with paneled reveals, side panels instead of sidelights, and transom above. The original porch is missing; a later partial replacement appears at the first floor entrance. The central door on the river side is flanked by two basement entrances to admit blocks of ice from the river. These were stored in an ice pit some thirty-seven feet deep and seventeen feet in diameter beneath the basement floor. Window lintels on the south and west faces are smooth and flat in the Classic manner. Those on the street side are segmental arches in brick.

David Cummins was probably the original owner. Subsequent deed holders included Jesse Whitehead, West Madison School, and Stanley Olmstead. J. Richard and Nancy Jones now own the building.

61. Brandt "Balloon Frame" House

A jump in tax value in 1842 indicates the erection of this building at 211 West Second Street in that year or the previous year. The property was owned from 1818 until 1865 by Felix Brandt and his heirs.

In the early 1830s lumber was already becoming scarce, and the wasteful construction method which

Frank S. Baker

had prevailed in New England, using heavy corner posts and heavy beams with equally heavy braces, gave way to a lighter method of construction known as the "balloon frame." This method was invented by George Washington Snow in Chicago in 1832 and soon became the most prevalent form of American light timber construction.[12] The Brandt house was erected in this new fashion, having hollow walls from floor to ceiling. Cubic in form, the house was weatherboarded and displays a plain cornice at the eaves, gable ends facing east and west, and windows that are four over four. The windows on the first story front extend to the floor. The vertical muntins are much

heavier than the horizontal ones, and the glass panels are very long for their width.

The Classic influence is demonstrated by the entablature-like member of the cornice, the floor-length windows, and the straight and plain window caps. The wood lintels show carved decorations in leaf forms which are higher in the center and taper in scrolls to both ends. However, the window caps are supported by corbels that show the influence of the Italian style. Curtis Jacobs is the present owner.

62. Hendricks-Smith House

In this house at 618 West Main Street the styles vary with the periods of construction, starting in 1837 with Federal and merging into Classic, with later Italianate embellishments. The Classic style is indicated in the fanlights and sidelights of the entrance. The red glass in the fanlight and the frosted glass in the sidelights

Frank S. Baker

12. Newcomb, *Architecture of the Old Northwest Territory*, 94–95.

represent later Victorian additions that took place when red glass was "all the rage." The Classic style is manifest in the portico with the Ionic columns and dentils, although this portico was probably a later addition. Brackets with pendants represent Italianate additions, as does the bay on the west side. The fence is identical with that at the Shrewsbury house, which was designed by Francis Costigan from sources in Asher Benjamin's design books. William Hendricks, Jr. (1809–50), an attorney, a state legislator, and county probate judge, initially held this property. Alden Smith was a later owner. John and Linda Dietrich now own it.

63. Hill House

Frank S. Baker

This structure at 707 East Main Street has had many alterations and stands on the site of an earlier building which also extended into the area at the rear. This earlier structure was possibly built in the late 1820s or early 1830s and was largely removed after it had fallen into ruinous condition. The present house is late Classic, circa 1846, with Italianate ornamentation. The lyre design in the iron gate was popular in the mid-nineteenth century. The present owners are Marjorie and Peter Hill.

Robert Twente

64. Hughes House

Thomas Godman, a prominent pork packer, acquired this land in 1853, and the house, at 707 West Second Street, was probably built before 1857. Largely cubic, the house extends the full depth of the block to the next street, encompassing the large rooms facing the street and a series of service buildings toward the rear. Classic in design, the street face contains a recessed entrance surmounted by a cornice decorated with dentils and supported by scroll-shaped corbels. Windows on the first floor are now one over one and extend to the floor. The lower sashes of these windows are much taller than the upper sashes, indicating that the originals were six over nine. The window lintels are smooth stone and slightly pedimented. The house had many design elements added later: the cornice with Italianate brackets, the entrance door with an etched, frosted glass panel, and the octagon section on the east side, added by Richard Johnson, Sr., after he bought the house in 1886. Service buildings to the rear were likely added by successive owners and include stables, stable hand quarters, original sanitation facilities, tack room, and carriage house. Robert and Betty Hughes now own the property.

65. St. Michael's Avenue Houses

These two brick houses at 422 and 424 St. Michael's Avenue may well have been constructed at the same time, judging by the smooth window lintels and sills in both. Brick dentils have survived on the house to the right and may exist under a later Italianate cornice on the house to the left. Both houses were built to accommodate the slope of the hillside, with the result that one of them was raised above the sidewalk level. Windows, one over one, are obviously replacements. In both houses there is evidence that the front and rear portions were built at different times. The present owners are Dennis W. Lory of 422 and Elston and Ada Boldery of 424.

Frank S. Baker

66. Thomas-Hare House

Frank S. Baker

In this large brick house at 400 Thomas Hill Road only the east rooms, one on the first floor and one on the second floor, and the halls are early, built probably in the 1830s. The brick was made on the site. The remaining sections of the house were added at various times over the years. The house is built on the solid stone of the hillside. Basil Bently in all probability was the initial owner. Subsequent owners included John R. Thomas. Francis and Marjorie Hare now own the property.

67. Stewart House

This house at 415 West Second Street has the mass and general Classic proportions that suggest it was constructed in the 1840s with Italianate details affixed in the 1870s. The broad gable, smooth, wide door casings, and windows, six over six and short, are also of Classic derivation. The heavy bracketed cornice and heavy window caps indicate a later Italianate influence. There is a hexagonal ornament in the tympanum of the pediment. An upper side porch under the main roof has a molded panel, indicating, perhaps, that a balustrade once existed there. Originally frame, the house is now covered with a modern fabric. The middle window in the set of three on the front facade is also a later addition. Lena Stewart owns the house at present.

Robert Twente

Frank S. Baker

68. White-Cofield House

The architect James White built this house at 410 Broadway for his residence in 1874. He acquired the property in three separate purchases: from John Northcraft for $525; from L. M. Noble for $705 in November, 1873; and from George Northcraft for $100 in November, 1873. The style of the house reflects the interest of the builder and not the period in which it was built. This fact explains the Classic elements that would be expected in the 1840s instead of the 1870s. This house is one of the few original frame buildings of any size remaining in town.

Cornices terminate in narrow pilasters at the corners of the building. The eaves are not boxed in but are supported by rafter brackets, as mentioned by A. J. Downing in his designs for country houses.[13] The windows on the front face are not equidistant and are two over two. The door with its elliptical fanlight above and sidelights has been moved to its present location from its original position on the south face. Elizabeth Mitchell once owned the real estate. Sidney and Margie Cofield now own it.

69. Classic Double Cottage

This brick Classic cottage at 411–13 Cragmont was built between 1832 and 1846 for two occupants. It has a door and a window on the front face of each half. From a foundation of stone the front wall rises to a three-step projecting cornice at the top. There are segmental arches in the brick above the windows. Timothy and Kathie Brooks presently own the cottage.

Frank S. Baker

13. Andrew Jackson Downing, *The Architecture of Country Houses* (1850; reprint, New York: Da Capo Press, 1968), 163, 279, 311.

Frank S. Baker

71. Kikendall-Bramwell House

Frank S. Baker

70. Watson House

This brick cottage at 625 Broadway is a simple statement of Classic proportions, in all likelihood built in the early 1840s. It faces the street with two windows toward one end of the front and a door and window toward the opposite end. The entire front is surmounted by brick dentils and an otherwise unornamented cornice. The entrance door has a four-panel transom but is a replacement. Shutters, heavy and obviously original, have survived. James and Lucy Watson now own the house.

South of the Bramwell house on Highway 7 north of Madison, the first structure on the west side of the road is described by Peat as a Classic cottage "chaste in its simplicity and restraint."[14] It was built between 1832 and 1846. The front door is flush with the wall of the house and has two windows on either side. There are no windows in the ends of the building.

This house was the last stop for drovers driving their livestock on foot through the woods from the north. They would then drive them down through the town of Madison and on to riverboats for shipping mostly to New Orleans. There were corrals at the back of the house where drovers would keep their livestock until a boat was in and ready to receive a cargo. The livestock might have come from as far as Indianapolis, Lafayette, Kokomo, or Michigan City. There was an occasional notice in the newspaper that, when a drove of hogs had been driven through the streets to the boat, two or three pigs had been lost coming through town. Samuel Kikendall originally owned the house. The present owners are Carter and Mary Bramwell.

14. Wilbur Peat, *Indiana Houses of the Nineteenth Century* (Indianapolis: Indiana Historical Society, 1962), 46.

72. Multiple House

Frank S. Baker

Main Street entrance, from an old photograph
Flora Collection, Indiana State Library

This two-story multiple at 727–35 West Third Street was originally a two-family house facing Main Street but with the rear close to Third Street. The entrances facing Main Street were Classic with pilasters, entablatures, straight transoms, sidelights, and slightly recessed doorways. The two-story bay in the east half is possibly a later addition. The roof is standing seam metal. The window lintels are smooth stone. There is one chimney in a dividing wall, and two others are bridged within the east wall, which

forms a fractable. The west half of the double was once lived in by the Garber family, who for many years published the Madison *Courier*. The present owners are William and Fauna Liter and James and Rosenell Breeding.

73. Morgan Apartment House

This six-apartment building, built on a very high, heavy stone foundation at 601 Mulberry Street, is basically Classic. According to Wilbur Peat, the entrance steps probably originally split into stairs going north and stairs going south, each starting from the same platform.[15] The cornice has dentils and modillions in the Classic style and a deep frieze in somewhat the manner of an entablature. Further Classical elements appear in the pilasters, in the sidelights of the entrance door, in the divided

Jack Boucher

15. Conversation with John T. Windle.

transoms above the door and sidelights, and in the cornice which tops the entrance. The building is nicely balanced and symmetrical in the best Classic manner. It is now under the ownership of Mary Louise Morgan.

74. Early Medical School

The house at 502 East Street is basically Classic and was built prior to 1853. Although it is largely lacking in ornamental details that can be attributed to any one style, the wide, smooth window frames are definitely Classic. The windows on the lower level are longer than those on the upper level but do not extend to the floor. Glass has long since been updated, and panes are now one over one. According to newspaper columnist Charles Heberhart, in 1852 and 1853 a group of doctors decided to establish a medical school in Madison.[16] The school utilized this two-story frame house as a classroom and the one-story brick building next door as a dissecting room. Three months after it opened a severe epidemic of cholera and an epidemic of typhoid struck the town; this building became a hospital, and the little brick building became a pest house. Roland Halcomb is the present owner.

Frank S. Baker

75. Eleutherian College

HMI

The Eleutherian College on State Road 250 at Lancaster was established in 1848 by Thomas Craven and others. It was one of the first integrated and coeducational colleges west of the Alleghenies. Constructed in the Classic style, the building is noted for the superb stonework in the walls. Semi-dressed quoins at the corners are plumb-line vertical. A cornice of wood is without ornament except for a small projecting molding. Dressed stones serve as window caps, again without ornament. Window sashes are original, with six panes over six. Two sets of doors at the entrance have transoms and flat stone caps. The belfry is louvered and contains a bell which is inscribed: "J. A. Kelley Franklin Brass and Bell Foundry, Madison." The original roof was in place when the building was given to Historic Madison, Inc., in 1973 by the family of Major T. Jester. That

16. Madison *Daily Courier*, 10 November 1939.

roof was composed of sheets of iron more than a quarter of an inch thick and about eight by ten feet square. Sections of the original plaster walls were troweled to excessive smoothness and painted black to serve as blackboards in the classrooms. Seats for students were made in groups, one attached to another, and are similar to those in the famous boys' school in Deerfield, Massachusetts. A lecture hall with a balcony at the rear occupies the first two floors along with the entrance foyer and staircases. Two huge cast-iron, wood-burning stoves located in the assembly hall provided the heat for the entire building.

Robert Twente

76. St. Michael's Rectory

The earliest reference that has been found to the construction at 519 East Third Street of a rectory for St. Michael's Church is a notice in the Madison *Courier* of September 30, 1859, announcing a fire in the carpenter's shop across Third Street from the church which destroyed "the doors, window sash, and other material for the Priest's new house, attached to St. Michael's Church."[17] In the centennial sermon of September 16, 1937, Rev. P. A. Deery stated that the present rectory was built in 1864 when Father

17. Ibid., 30 September 1859. The carpenter's shop belonged to Mr. Herbst.

Dupontavice was pastor.[18] Therefore, construction of the rectory probably commenced before the date of the fire and finished in 1864.

In 1971 St. Michael's rectory was included in the Historic American Buildings Survey for Indiana. The HABS description gives the following information: "Stuccoed rubble stone with brick cornice, 34′2″ (three irregularly spaced bays) x 32′2″ (4 bays), 2 stories on sloping site with basement fully exposed on south, hipped roof, modified central hall plan. Built c. 1860 as priests' living quarters and offices. Forms complete church group with adjacent stone sanctuary and tower of St. Michael's." There is a large covered porch on the east side of the house and a small porch on the north side. On the first and second levels on the south side there are four six over six double-hung windows and two windows and two doors on the basement level. All the windows have heavy louvered shutters. In its mass and profile the priest's house at St. Michael's Church closely resembles the garden houses designed by the famous sixteenth-century Italian architect Giacomo da Vignola at Villa Lante about sixty miles north of Rome.

77. Madison United Presbyterian Church

Robert Twente

Reminiscent of the early churches in New England, this church at 202 Broadway is built in a restrained Classic style. An architect by the name of Humes designed the structure, which went up in 1848. A projecting tower pierces the entablature and cornice of the front facade. The face of the tower is broken by entrance doors at the top of a flight of steps. The wide entablature is surmounted by a rather plain projecting cornice which extends the length of the sidewalls. Pilasters at the corners and at intervals down the sidewalls divide the sidewalls into panels

18. Ibid., 30 September 1937.

containing windows, now stained glass but originally clear glass. The tower rises in three tiers. The bottom section is built of brick up to the cornice and to a point just slightly above the comb of the roof. The second section is a setback cube built of wood with corner pilasters, entablature, cornice, and four louvered openings. The topmost section, again set back, is octagonal with louvered openings, a denticulated cornice, and a bell-shaped roof.

The sanctuary is very high, and the walls are surmounted by a deep entablature with an extended ogee member that makes transitions into a flat, paneled ceiling. A low railing around the pulpit or chancel area encloses seats for the choir and also the console of the organ. Door casings are wide and flat without decoration. A gallery at the rear is entered by two staircases. The auditorium is above a high basement, which necessitates a great many steps from the street. These steps consist in part of the original stone.

Robert Twente

78. St. John's United Church of Christ

Originally constructed as St. John's Methodist Church in 1848–50 with the cornerstone laid in April of 1849, this building at 501 East Main Street is now St. John's United Church of Christ. Built on a low foundation, this small Classic structure has a gable end and pediment facing the street, windows with smooth dressed-stone lintels and sills, and stained glass that was added at a later date. The tympanum, or space within the pediment, contains a stone bearing the following inscription: "Deutsche Evang. Kirche Organisert 1842." Double doors with deep panels have brick pilasters at the sides, and there are pilasters from the ground to cornice at the corners of the building. Also, the church contains a small tracker organ.

79. First Baptist Church

Frank S. Baker

Located at 416 Vine Street, adjacent to the Christian Church's parking lot, the First Baptist Church occupies a building Classic in design with a high-ceilinged sanctuary, entered by stairs within the entrance at street level. Also at street level is a low-ceilinged room below the sanctuary. The street facade is deeply pedimented, and the entrance is surmounted by a pedimented cap. The windows, which are long and originally nine over nine on the upper floor and short and six over six below, are fitted into vertical panels made by brick pilasters which run the full height of the building. These pilasters are surmounted by a heavy cornice decorated with dentils at the top of the frieze and well-defined Classic moldings. The window treatment and cornice are the same on the sidewalls as on the front.

According to a pamphlet published by the First Baptist Church, Jesse Vawter organized the church in Madison in 1807. He built a log church on top of the hill, which he called Mt. Pleasant, near his home, which he called Mt. Glad. In 1831 the congregation decided to move downtown to Vine Street. The Vine Street church was destroyed in 1850. This new building was started in 1853 and finished in 1860.

John Hopkins of the Historic American Buildings Survey has found moldings in the church similar to those used by Dubach in the courthouse in 1854, leading him to believe in Dubach's involvement in the church design.

80. Jefferson County Courthouse

The Jefferson County Courthouse, designed by architect David Dubach in the Classic Revival style and built in 1854–55, replaced an earlier building which burned in 1853. The cost was $36,000.

The lower floor exterior is rusticated, and the west facade is pierced by three large round arches. Above these arches stands an Ionic tetrastyle portico. Windows are long, and those on the street sides are capped with slightly projecting stone lintels supported by corbels. The building is surmounted by a very large dome and cupola. In the dome is a bell weighing 3,116 pounds and a town clock installed by Israel Fowler, a Madison clockmaker. The stone came from Marble Hill, a few miles south of Madison. At that time it was believed that this stone was a fine grade of marble, but it was quickly discovered that Marble Hill stone eroded easily unless kept painted. During an extensive remodeling in 1960 the two-story courtroom was sacrificed to

provide an additional floor, but the exterior architecture was not altered.

Pediments appear on all four sides of the building. Dubach seems to have altered these pediments during construction. He doubled the elevation of the pediments and possibly made the columns a bit slimmer than his original drawing indicates.

The Madison courthouse shows many similarities in design with the courthouse plan shown in Lafever's *Young Builder's General Instructor*. These similarities indicate that Dubach had a copy of the Lafever book in his possession at the time the Madison structure was built.[19] The dome, entablature, and cornices are similar. The pediment in Lafever is flatter and more Greek, thus more like the Dubach drawing, and Dubach's pediment as built is steeper and more Roman.

According to a newspaper report of 1859, after a fire in 1858 John Temperly was in charge of replacing the courthouse cupola.[20]

19. Minard Lafever, *The Young Builder's General Instructor, Containing the Five Orders of Architecture* (Newark, N.J.: Tuttle and Company, 1829), plate 59.
20. Madison *Daily Courier*, 18 April 1859.

81. Jefferson County Jail and Sheriff's House

The present structure on the courthouse square is the third jail on this site. The first was of logs, and the second, built in the 1830s, was replaced by the present building, which was accepted by the commissioners in September, 1849. It has a recessed doorway in the Classic tradition, a low-pitched roof, gable end facing the street, and a Classic pediment. The walls of the present building were constructed by McKim and Falkner of stone from the Vernon quarry in Jennings County. In the cellblock portion at the rear the walls are three to four feet thick and contain single stones as large as bathtubs. The walls of the front portion of the building are brick as is the cornice. The ceiling of the cellblock is vaulted. The original gutters drained water from the roof through depressions cut into the stone to form channels. The jail has been kept intact, with its heavy iron doors, heavy chains, and very large locks on dungeon-like cells. The key to the main door is more than a foot long.

HABS/HAER

HABS/HAER

HABS/HAER

V

Gothic Revival

IT WAS THE ROMANTIC movement that swept across Europe and the British Isles during the end of the eighteenth and beginning of the nineteenth centuries that inspired the Gothic Revival in architecture. Protesting the formalism of the Classic mode, its proponents turned to the medieval churches for their models. "Christian Architecture," as it was called by the English architect Augustus W. N. Pugin, became the accepted style for ecclesiastical buildings. Ironically, it was Thomas Jefferson and Benjamin Henry Latrobe, those champions of Classic style, who first introduced the Gothic mode to America. Even before the Revolution Jefferson proposed the erection of a Gothic garden temple, and in 1799–1800 Latrobe designed and erected the first great house in the Gothic manner at "Sedgely," an estate near Philadelphia.

Numerous books have been written on the Gothic Revival by architectural historians. John Poppeliers and his associates have written one of the most succinct descriptions of the characteristics of this style in their volume entitled *What Style Is It ?*:

Gothic Revival was distinguished by the pointed arch that could ingeniously be combined with towers, crenellation, steep gabled roofs, lacy bargeboards, bay and oriel windows, tracery and leaded stained glass. House plans were asymmetrical to allow flexibility in arrangement of rooms and create picturesque external silhouettes.[1]

In the United States church architecture conformed more closely to the medieval than did domestic architecture. Madison possesses two such examples: St. Michael's Catholic Church and Christ Episcopal Church.

According to Rexford Newcomb, "Indiana may have been later in adopting the Gothic vogue, but, by the same token, her earlier efforts were more authentic." He cites Christ Episcopal Church as "an excellent Gothic design" and mentions that its architect, W. Russell West, also designed the Ohio Capitol.[2]

A third church in Madison, Trinity United Methodist, built in 1873, is likewise in the Gothic mode but represents a later development known as Neo-Gothic, popular in the last quarter of the nineteenth century and well into the twentieth.

It was not until the 1830s that the Gothic developed as a national domestic style that continued through and after the Civil War era. The popular appeal of this style was largely generated by the romantic writings of Lord Byron and Sir Walter Scott, whose novels and poems based on medieval legends captured the spirit of the Gothic and the imaginations of architects and the general public. However, the publication and wide distribution of carpenters' handbooks made it a practical and popu-

1. John Poppeliers, S. Allen Chambers, and Nancy B. Schwartz, *What Style Is It?* (Washington: The Preservation Press of the National Trust for Historic Preservation, 1977), 18.
2. Rexford Newcomb, *Architecture of the Old Northwest Territory: A Study of Early Architecture in Ohio, Indiana, Illinois, Michigan, Wisconsin, and Part of Minnesota* (Chicago: University of Chicago Press, 1950), 141.

lar mode in cities, towns, and rural areas across the country. Preeminent among these writers of guides and handbooks was Andrew Jackson Downing, who published the designs of Alexander Jackson Davis, the chief exponent of the Gothic style in the mid-nineteenth century. Although Davis is probably best known for his design of Lyndhurst (1838) near Tarrytown, New York, now a property of the National Trust, his designs for the country cottage popularized the Gothic style for the small American home.

Wilbur Peat, contrasting the Classic and Gothic modes, notes: "No longer are the words pediment, entablature, portico...applicable.... For analysis of Gothic architecture we turn to such terms as gable, bargeboard, tracery, and cresting...."[3]

The four types of domestic architecture in the Gothic mode, as defined by Peat, are well represented in Madison: 1) a simple rectangular block with a roof of normal pitch and with an acute-angled gable attached to the main roof on the side; 2) the type without extensions or ells and with the entrance in the gable; 3) the type similar to plan two but with matching gables left and right; and 4) the L-shaped plan with a porch in the angle and the door opening out onto the porch.[4]

Of the decorative elements the most widely used in the smaller houses in Madison was the bargeboard, sometimes referred to as the vergeboard or gableboard. It is a board which hangs from the projecting end of a roof, covers the gables, and is often carved and ornamented. Bargeboards were hung on both one-story and two-story houses in Madison, as elsewhere. Originally, they were cut out in patterns of openwork by hand chisel, but the work was quickly taken over by the scroll saw, which

became available in the mid-thirties. The saw, powered by steam, simplified the process greatly, although to Andrew Jackson Downing it had one disadvantage. He complained that the jigsaw made it possible to use thin boards that looked flimsy instead of heavy boards that were cut out by a chisel. Both types were used in Madison, and both will be illustrated in the following pages. Some of the boards are exact duplicates, but there are also many patterns that were obviously the work of original designers and occurred in only one or a few instances. The shape of the capital "S" was a favorite design among the cutters. Sometimes the "S" faced in one direction, and sometimes, in the opposite. Sometimes it had cusps or slightly curved projections along its external perimeter. The bargeboard underwent considerable evolution, becoming first more florid and elaborate and rather large and bold. Later a conservative trend reduced it to a smaller geometric pattern. This pattern showed a slight elaboration of the line of the eave on a gable end, was straight and narrow, and sometimes had only a curl at its lower terminus. For a city of its size, Madison has undoubtedly one of the most comprehensive collections of bargeboards that has survived any place in the United States. More than forty individual designs have been counted in the city, and more than eighty-five buildings have been so decorated.

Other eave decorations in the Gothic mode include swags attached to the verge of the eave, extending only part way down the rake of the gable. Also made with the scroll saw, these decorations often include turned and carved pieces.

3. Wilbur Peat, *Indiana Houses of the Nineteenth Century* (Indianapolis: Indiana Historical Society, 1962), 85–86.
4. Ibid., 86–87.

Still another modification of the eave decoration which appears with some frequency in Madison is that of the triangle which fills the space at the peak of the gable. This board panel pierced with openings in decorative patterns was again done largely by the scroll saw. It occasionally appears in combination with shingles on the main wall of the house. These shingles are shaped sometimes in the fishtail and fish scale patterns and sometimes with chamfered corners. The wood triangles occur in some of the same houses that have bargeboards but more frequently on houses without further decorations, except possibly wood lace around the top of a porch.

Of the decorative elements of Gothic Revival architecture in Madison, next to the bargeboard probably the most visible is wood lace, commonly known as carpenters' lace. Some of the components of wood lace are wood turnings made on a lathe. There are spindles and balls threaded on spindles. These may be set in rows and may span the entire front of a house, sometimes interspersed with cutout areas done on a jigsaw.

82. St. Michael's Catholic Church

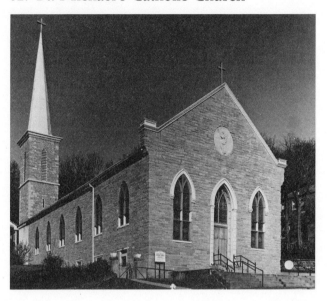

Frank S. Baker

The land for this church at 519 East Third Street was given by John McIntyre in two lots in 1837 and 1838. According to statements published by St. Michael's, the "sandstone of which the church is constructed was hauled by ox teams from the railroad cut which had been started in 1837. It was the following year that work was begun on St. Michael's."[5] The church was completed a few days before Christmas in 1839 and prepared for dedication. Among the pioneer parishioners was "Francis Costigan, the reputed architect of the church."[6] The Register of Baptisms of the parish lists the baptism of Costigan's son on August 24, 1838, and of his wife, Eliza, on April 21, 1839.

The church is Gothic, built of partially dressed stone. Windows on the main floor have a pointed

5. *St. Michael's Church, Madison Indiana* (n.p., n.d.), 2.
6. Charles F. Walsh, comp., *St. Michael's Church, Madison, Indiana: A Pioneer Parish of Southern Indiana, 1817–1937* (n.p., 1937), 28.

Frank S. Baker

arch head with intersecting tracery and leaded stained glass. The ones on the south facade have metal hood moldings painted to resemble stone. Above the main entrance a carved stone roundel replaces an earlier stained glass and lead rose window. The roof is a very low pitch, not characteristic of the Gothic style. It was the kind of roof with which Costigan was familiar and indicated his background and Classic training. In designing the roof Costigan produced a ceiling using the form of the double curve, sometimes referred to as the "open book" design.

In 1865 newspapers carried announcements of the building of a vestry and plans to build a steeple.[7] Having the tower at the rear of the church is sufficiently unusual to have warranted special mention over the years. An octagonal, wood-frame spire covered with copper rises on the stone tower base. The tower contains four hanging bells in the sizes forty-two, thirty-six, and twenty-four inches. They were made by the Hy. Stuckstede Foundry Company of St. Louis, Missouri, and were donated in 1895 and 1911. Another bell which is in the tower, but not hanging, is inscribed "Cincinnati, Ohio, 1846."

83. Christ Episcopal Church

The Christ Episcopal Church at 506 Mulberry Street is another of the early examples of the Gothic style in this part of the country. Built in 1848, it has the steep roof, the small buttresses, the pointed arches, and the exposed beams and rafters characteristic of Gothic interpretation.

The building committee of the church requested Cincinnati architect W. Russell West to make plans similar to St. John's Episcopal Church in Louisville. He was paid thirty dollars for designing the building. Matthew Temperly was given the contract to superintend the construction; a Mr. Hinds was chosen to do the brickwork; and a Mr. Benneman, the stonework. A bell was ordered from Messrs. Meenley and Sons of Troy, New York. An organ in a Gothic case to correspond with the church's interior was purchased in 1851 from Mathias Schwab Organ Company of Cincinnati, and a tubular carillon was presented by Arthur Orr of Chicago. The architect, West, designed the iron fence which was made by a Mr. Torrance in Madison at a cost of $2.75 per foot, not including the locks. The cornerstone of the church was laid on October 31, 1848, and the dedication service held on February 7, 1850. It is estimated that the building cost $7,500 to construct.

7. Madison *Daily Courier*, 19 August 1865.

84. St. Mary's Catholic Church

St. Mary's Catholic Church at 413 East Second Street was constructed in 1850–51 and is Gothic in style. The church is built of brick and has pointed arches in the windows and above the doors. A square tower is centered on the front with pilasters at the corners. A wooden bell chamber, octagonal with louvered openings, rises above the tower. The steeple was erected and chimes installed in 1860. Small pointed gables at the eight corners of the bell tower flank the sharply pointed spire. In 1888 the church was refrescoed, and cathedral glass replaced the common window glass.

HABS/HAER

The following article appeared in the Madison *Daily Courier* of August 23, 1850:

THE NEW GERMAN CATHOLIC CHURCH ON SECOND STREET, BETWEEN WALNUT AND EAST STREETS. The corner-stone of this church will be laid on Sunday the 25th inst., at five o'clock in the afternoon, with all the imposing ceremonies of the Catholic Church. A sermon in the German language will be preached by the Rev. Joseph Rudolph, and one in English by the Rev. Pastor of the Irish Catholic congregation of this city.

The church is to be built in the Gothic style; 45 feet front, by 100 feet deep, and about 40 feet high; under the superintendence of Mr. Grainer, architect.

85. Trinity United Methodist Church

This church, a structure of Gothic influence, is not Gothic Revival but really Neo-Gothic, with various elements of design applied which in no way are functional. It is located at 409 Broadway, between Main and Third streets.

The cornerstone was laid on September 9, 1872, and the building was dedicated in June, 1874. The first service held in the building, before it was finished, was a marriage ceremony on September 26, 1873.

Records are scant, but tradition has the name of B. V. Enos and Son of Indianapolis as the firm that designed the building and supervised construction. A newspaper item, however, noted that Robert McKim, a local furniture manufacturer, consented to superintend the construction.[8] The material of the building is brick on a stone foundation, with stone arches and trimmings. The cornices, pinnacle on the turret, the finial of the spire, and other moldings were fabricated of galvanized iron by John Adams. The foundation

8. Ibid., 6 July 1872.

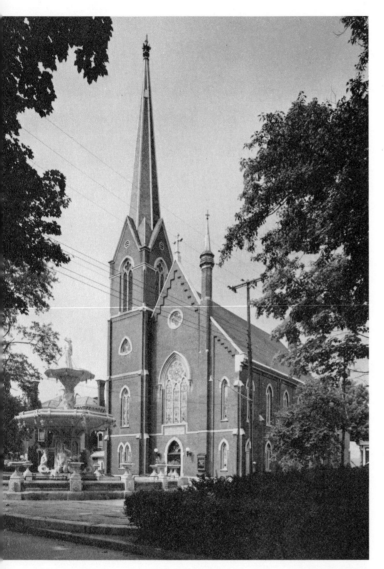

HABS/HAER

work was done by Samuel Liffitt; the brickwork, by James Dorsey; the stone trim, by James Crozier and John Jager; and the steeple construction, by John Eckert. The cost of the building was $30,606. Acoustical problems led to the construction of ornamental beams in the sanctuary. A tracker organ was installed around 1898. The stained glass windows were supplied by W. Coulter and Son of Cincinnati between 1900 and 1905.

86. Ebenezer Methodist Church

The dating of this building at 409 Poplar Street is difficult due to the scarcity of historical information. It is known from newspaper reports that in 1867 and 1868 the Ebenezer congregation, having for some years worshiped in a house on Walnut Street, purchased an old brick carpenter's shop on the site of the present church and with the help of the Freedmen's Bureau fitted it up as a church and school.[9] A decade later, in 1878, according to a published history of Madison Methodism, the black congregation tore down the carpenter's shop and erected a new church at the same location.[10]

Frank S. Baker

9. Ibid., 29 May 1867; 4 December 1868.
10. Rev. R. M. Barnes, D.D., and Rev. W. W. Snyder, A.M., *Historic Sketches of the Methodist Episcopal Church in Madison, Indiana* (Madison, 1903), 94–131.

That a new building actually went up is controverted by the evidence of the existing architecture. There are enough extant Classic elements — brick dentils, pilasters, and segmental arched windows — to suggest that the carpenter's shop is still there, and that it was built between 1835 and 1855. The Gothic features in the windows and entrance door, meanwhile, indicate a later remodeling. Thus, it is possible that the church was unable to find the means for rebuilding and simply updated the old structure with Gothic embellishments.

87. Second Baptist Church

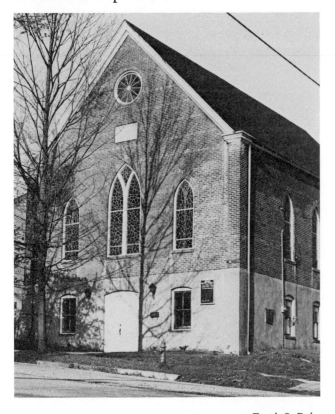

Frank S. Baker

In May of 1883 the black Baptists of Madison, under the leadership of Rev. J. C. Dorsey, purchased a lot at what is now 611 Broadway on which to erect a new church building. The firm of Rankin and White received the contract for its construction and groundbreaking took place in August, 1883. The cost of the building was around $4,000.[11]

This Gothic building of stone and brick has a pointed gable toward the street and a two-pitch roof. The first level is stone with a stucco surface. The upper portion is brick. The entrance is at ground level and has an inside staircase. Pilasters at the corners of the building rise through the full height and are topped with projecting caps. Two Gothic pointed windows enclosed within a single pointed arch surmount the entrance and are flanked by a single pointed window on either side. These windows are encased within a pointed Gothic arch in the brick wall. In the top of the gable a round window containing radiating mullions dividing the glass into twelve panes pierces the wall. The windows on the side walls duplicate those in the front facade.

11. Madison *Daily Courier*, 11 May 1883; 12 May 1883; 22 August 1883.

88. Carpenters' Lace House

Built probably before 1866, this house at 738 West Third Street with its porch of elaborate wood lace is a fine example of Steamboat Gothic. A frieze across the top of the porch contains bands of designs cut out with a scroll saw, brackets, corbels, and turned spindles with wooden balls threaded on them. The frieze is supported by thin turned posts with cutout brackets flaring into the horizontal bands. A pointed gable in the middle of a low-pitched roof faces the street. The peak of the gable is filled with a wood panel containing perforated openings made by a scroll saw. Like so many other fences in town the one on this property has posts made by Cobb and Stribling, and the decorative pattern of the gate is also prevalent. Michael Bright was probably the original owner. Barbara and Robert Walters presently own the house.

89. "Carriage House"

Originally located on the north side of Main Street behind the Haigh house, which occupied the present location of the Madison Clinic, this carriage house is now behind the Trolley Barn on West Main Street. It displays many of the characteristics of the late bargeboard Gothic, with mixtures from other preceding styles, including the hip roof of the third phase

HABS/HAER

90. Dr. Kremer Office

In this brick cottage at 324 East Second Street the reduced bargeboard with ogee decorations at the ends and brackets to the building would indicate a late modification in the bargeboard period. The gable end of the building faces Second Street and contains a circular ventilator framed in brick. The long side of the building on Walnut Street is interrupted by a

Frank S. Baker

Frank S. Baker

of the Classic and also of the Georgian and the cupola which was found in the Georgian and again in the Classic. The roof was initially of slate with patterns made in colors, but it was replaced with other material when the building was moved to its present location. The gable toward the street is surmounted by a triangle of pierced, decorated wood and has a finial and pendant. Bargeboards appear not only on the gables but also around the eaves between the gables. The roof on the end gables is hipped. The carriage doors and hay door above have Roman arches, and the carriage doors have heavy X-shaped supports with chamfered edges. Similar X-shaped supports for carriage doors appear in other buildings of the same date in the city. The cupola is square and louvered and supports a high, pointed roof with an ornament at the peak. Iron stars in the exterior walls are attached to iron tie rods which cross the width of the building and control the outward pressure.

J. F. Bruning, a dry goods merchant, first owned the property. Sidney E. Haigh, superintendent of the Madison Woolen Mills, held the deed later. The present owner is Kendra Leininger.

gable of sharper pitch, conforming to the usual pattern for houses of this style. The transom over the Second Street door is ornamented with designs in colored glass, showing a mortar and pestle on the one side and a graduated measuring glass on the other. The center panel is etched with the name "Dr. Kremer." All parts are set off with lead. On the length of the slate roof near the eave there is a snow board set at an angle, which serves to keep snow from sliding off the roof. It is supported at intervals by ogee-like blocks. Dr. Kremer lived in the house next door and used this small building as his office from sometime between 1903 and 1907 until 1947.

91. Wilson-Stookey House

Same design in reverse, 818-20 East Second

Frank S. Baker

Frank S. Baker

When John Paul died in 1835, lot 14 of the first addition west of the city was sold to Joseph Wilson for forty-six dollars through the executor William Hendricks. This lot came from three proprietors: J. Burnet, one quarter part for twenty dollars; Lewis Davis, one quarter part for twenty-five dollars; and William Hendricks, one half part for one dollar. Statements in the tax records of 1837 and 1839 indicate the existence of a house on the lot. In 1854 Wilson sold the east fraction of the lot to James G. Wright for $1,000.

The frame house at 308 West Second Street on that lot has a porch tucked under the gable on its east side. It has a prominent bargeboard that would classify in the wavy line group with kerfs. The same design in reverse is seen on the house at 818–20 East Second Street. Joseph Wilson originally owned the house. Charles and Alice Stookey are the present owners.

Bargeboards and Gable Ends

Photographs by Frank S. Baker

Heavy, Hand-Cut Bargeboards

933-35 West Second

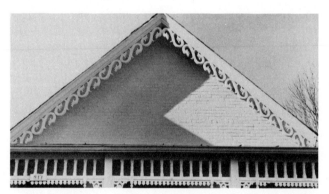

811 Walnut

118 West Fifth

Thinner, Scroll-Sawed Variations

315-17 Cragmont

714 East First

318 East Fourth

Elaborate Modifications, Thin and Scroll Sawed

Scallops and Pendants

920 East Second

701 Elm

804 East First

707 Elm

208 East Second

749-51 West Main

Three Variations on the Wave Design

503 East Main

321 Cragmont

712 East Second

More Variations from the Scroll Saw

633 Broadway

208 Lincoln

421-23 Mill

More Variations

107 East Second

724-26 West Third

215 East

408 Presbyterian

Related Designs

212 Baltimore

116 Jefferson

115 St. Michael's

Pendant Borders, Valance Type

613 East Main

507 Jefferson

713-15 West Main

915 West First

505 East Main

909 Walnut

513 East

Loops and Waves

219 West Fifth

1007 West Main

111-13 St. Michael's

Geometric Variants

620 West Second

721 West Third

417-19 Mill

Gable Ends

Scroll-Sawed Peak Decorations

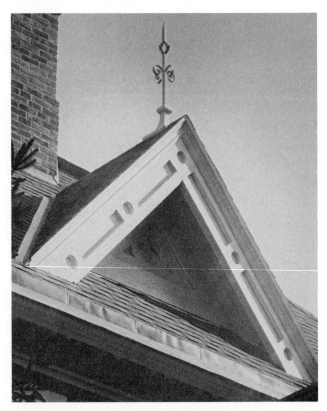

Angles and lines, late, 513 West Main

414 East Fourth

129 Mulberry

Swags and wood lace, 214 East First

Scroll-Sawed and Turned Peak Decorations

936 West Main

606 West Third

Gable End Variants

622 Broadway

924 East Second

504 East Second

Gable End Ventilators

Scroll-sawed and turned, 506 East Main

VI

Italianate

JUST AS THE CLASSIC Revival had its origins in ancient Greece and Rome, so the Italianate or Tuscan had its roots in the rural architecture of medieval and Renaissance Italy. Brought from England to the United States in the 1830s and modified to adapt to our climate and to the building materials available, the Italianate style achieved great popularity through and following the Civil War years. Again the plans of Alexander Jackson Davis, circulated in Andrew Jackson Downing's books, helped to popularize the style. Although there are still many examples of the Italianate in domestic architecture in Madison, the greatest number of these structures can be seen in the Main Street business area. This increased density is due to a series of fires in that section of the town in the 1860s and 1870s which necessitated rebuilding at a time when the Italianate style was at its height of popularity.

The most visible features of this style which appear in downtown Madison are these: ornaments embellishing brick buildings, extended eaves supported by brackets, and capped window lintels either in cut or carved stone or of pressed sheet-metal that has been formed to give the appearance of stone. Most local store buildings are at least two stories high, and some, even three. Originally, the first story usually had thin cast-iron Greek columns, very delicate in scale, that often had small capitals with acanthus leaves. Between the columns the fronts were made of wood panels and glass windows. Window panes were divided into relatively large sections, sometimes eighteen to twenty-four inches wide and up to forty inches high. Plate glass in large sheets was not yet available, but glassmakers had learned to produce somewhat larger sections than they had previously. Walls above the first floor were made of brick. Windows were tall and narrow with heavily ornamented caps. Bracketed cornices finished the top of the building. It was the period of the greatly flattened roof, its low pitch draining at the rear of the building. The heavy cornice at the top of the front wall was frequently attached to a parapet which extended above the functional part of the top floor.

Most of the examples of this style remaining on Main Street have been altered on the first floor and have lost their cast-iron columns in the process. Some few, however, have remained untouched, while some others have merely been encased within a surface of other materials of modern origin. In a few cases these latter have had modern materials removed, revealing the original facade.

Some of the best examples which survive include Wheeler's Barber Shop, the building at 110 West Main Street, and the Cisco-Auxier building.

92. "Eggleston" House

This house at 419 Broadway extends deep on the lot along Third Street to the alley. It then stretches along the alley so that the outbuildings are connected to the house. On the front of the house is a porch with elaborate iron decorations under a wood cornice showing dentils. The block of the brick house carries an Italian cornice decorated with sawtooth trim, brackets, and modillions. The windows on the first level go to the floor and are two over two. On the second level the windows in the front are two over two. In the back of the house the windows are nine over six. The house contains a good example of trompe l'oeil painting on the walls of the halls and a room toward the back of the house. It is similar to that formerly in the Levy-Swarts house.

According to tradition John Paul built the house for his daughter, Sarah Stevenson, who acquired possession of the property at the time of his death in 1836. Edward Eggleston, author of *The Hoosier Schoolmaster*, lived in this house between 1891 and 1902, toward the end of his life. It has been said that the sunroom on the south side of the house toward the front was added for him. The Goode family held the property at one time. The present owners are Thomas and Maryanne Imes.

93. Hendricks-Beall House

This house at 620 West Main Street was built between 1848 and 1858. It is an Italianate brick with central projection toward the street, small ells at the east and west sides, and lacy cast-iron porches in each of the corners formed by the ells. A large, imposing, cast-iron, balcony-like, roofed porch, entered only from the house, spans the front of the house, and above it, at the eaves, is a heavy, ornate, Italian cornice with brackets and dentils. The windows on the first level are floor length, six over nine, and usable as doors. The first owner of the house was William Hendricks. William Stapp acquired it later. Hilary Beall owns it at present.

HABS/HAER

HABS/HAER

94. Newell House-Girls' Club

Frank S. Baker

The 1842 construction date for this house at 109 West Third Street comes from Mrs. H. Newell, the wife of the builder.[1] However, the Italian decorations, including the cornices, window caps, and door casing in pressed metal, must have been added at a somewhat later date, when pressed metal came into vogue and was being added to many of the houses and storefronts.

This house is brick and has similarities to the "Eggleston" house on the southwest corner of Broadway and Third. Both have cornices which return for a short distance on gable ends, brackets and modillions in the cornices, sawtooth molding in the frieze, and denticulated window caps. The corbels supporting the window caps vary slightly in the two houses. The entrance door of the Newell house has corbels which differ from those on the windows but which conform closely to the scroll design found in many other houses. The slightly pedimented cap over the door and the door jambs is metal. Windows are two over two, and the lower ones on the front extend to the floor and are engaged with the stone band at the top of the foundation. The Girls' Club of Jefferson County now holds this property.

95. Monfort-Collins and Lewis-Ary Houses

These two houses are sufficiently similar in style to warrant describing the one to the east (left) at 921 West Main Street and then noting only the obvious differences between it and the one to the west at 923 West Main Street. Both houses appear to have been constructed in the early 1850s. The front portion of the first house, projecting toward the street, is brick with an L-shaped frame portion to the rear and porches filling the area within the ell under the roof of the front gable. The upstairs porch is enclosed by a balustrade topped by a plain molding with balusters turned between squared tops and bottoms. Skirting at the top of the porch is elaborate, with spindles and applied wood decorations in the Italian manner. Brick bases under the columns on the first floor porch are recent. The gable end toward the street has a projecting cornice supported by paired modillions. Front windows in the portion projecting toward the street are double, side by side, double-hung, single pane sashes on both floors. Windows are capped in pairs

1. Madison *Daily Courier*, 26 August 1885.

Robert Twente

by simple moldings that project only slightly. The Monfort family originally held title to this house, and the Brushfield family owned it later. E. A. and Lillian Collins are the present owners.

In the house toward the west the differences are chiefly in the windows in the front face, which are spaced two above and two below and at a considerable distance apart, and in the spindle wood turnings in the porch skirtings. The Lewis family initially owned the property. Allen Ary now owns it.

96. Robinson-Alcorn House

This brick Italianate house at 934 West Main Street was built in 1863 for Don Carlos Robinson, a local shipbuilder and subsequent proprietor of an extensive sawmill. It was restored in 1984. An Italianate cornice with brackets and sawtooth moldings surrounds a hip roof. The windows are capped with stone, slightly pedimented, but without further ornament. Windows are six over six, except for the two floor-length windows on the front, which are six over nine. A two-story bay occupies part of the east side. The porch is twentieth century. Merritt O., Merritt K., and George L. Alcorn are the present owners.

Frank S. Baker

97. Kelley House

Heavily Italianate in a manner which indicates that its style is due to original design rather than later additions, this house at 907 West Main Street is brick with windows that are two over two and framed with projecting caps supported by corbels. The four openings in the front wall and the chimneys in the end walls are balanced in the Classic manner, and the general proportions of the building show a holdover from the Classic period. It is owned by James and Mary Kelley.

Robert Twente

Frank S. Baker

98. Levy-Swarts House

The late Italianate style is well illustrated by this pre-1870 house at 705 West Second Street. The unusually heavy cornice has deeply carved brackets alternating with medallions. The roof is hipped and so low in pitch as to be invisible from the street. The entrance has outer double doors and a single inner door making a vestibule. The inner doorway has sidelights and frosted glass with designs; the outer doors have deeply molded wood panels. Windows on the front facade are arched with projecting and ornamental lintels. Inside shutters that fold back and are divided into upper and lower sections are complete throughout the house. The hall once contained trompe l'oeil painting similar to that in the "Eggleston" house. An advertisement offering this thirteen-room house for sale in 1878 listed a stable, wash house, woodshed, and coal house among the outbuildings, all of which have since disappeared.[2]

Sarah Levy first owned this house. Attorney Marcus Sulzer, who was mayor of Madison from 1926 to 1930 and from 1935 to 1939, lived in this house from 1899 to 1920. The present owners are Fred and Sandra Swarts.

2. Madison *Daily Evening Star*, 2 March 1878.

99. Trow-Thomas House

The brackets in the cornice and the two-story bay of this house at 403 West First Street are characteristic of the late Italian era. The two over two windows are probably original. The third-floor windows at the rear, which are also two over two and appear to be original, pierce the deep cornice at the top. The one over one windows and the iron portico facing First Street are replacements, as are some portions of the rear porches. The entire house is equipped with heavy shutters with movable louvers, which are probably original. When the house was built, the kitchen was located in the basement.

According to deed records, this property, in a subdivision of the estate of William Hendricks, was sold by Ann P. Hendricks in 1867 to Ellen C. Weyer for $1,200. This sum indicates that there was a building on the property at that time. The city directory of 1875 does not list the Weyers at this address, but the directory of 1879 shows that they were residing there. From this information one can assume that the house was substantially complete by that date. In 1882 the house was purchased from Ellen and Edward Weyer by Mary Trow for $5,000. It is presently owned by J. Brinton Thomas.

German Collection

100. Crawford-Johnson House

The abstract of this property at 601 West Second Street indicates that Samuel Crawford acquired it in 1854 for $960. In the city directory of 1859 he is listed as residing at this location. A newspaper of October, 1871, lists the property for sale with this description: "2 story brick residence on the southwest corner of Second and Vine. 10 rooms, kitchen, wood house, smoke house, &c., porches, 2 cisterns."[3] The property was sold in 1872 for $3,500. The rear portion of the house was built probably in the 1850s; the front part, probably in 1870–71.

Robert Twente

Large and generally cubic, the house displays many designs that are strongly Italianate. The roof, which is hipped as well as gabled, is crowned by delicate iron lacework which is mounted like a fence on the comb and which encircles a flat deck. A deeply recessed entrance is surrounded by panels decorated

3. Madison *Daily Courier*, 14 October 1871.

with geometric designs, and a single door contains heavily decorated leaded glass and is flanked by sidelights. The windows are well above floor level and are capped with plain, flush stone lintels. The exception is the middle window on the second floor, which is deeply hooded and further ornamented with pendant finials and wood lace. Windows in the gable ends on the third level have round tops. Most of the windows are shuttered. The eaves project deeply and are ornamented with brackets and pendant finials. Ornamental triangles in the peaks of the gables bear superimposed carvings. Cast-iron faces on either side of the front entrance are recent additions salvaged from the old fountain on Broadway. Richard and Pauline Johnson now own the house.

Frank S. Baker

101. Kirk House

This Italianate brick house at 613 West Main Street was built by Alexander White and Robert Rankin in 1869–70. It is a story and a half with sharply pitched gables. In the front of the house, first story windows extend to the floor and have flush, smooth, stone lintels. A triple window in the front gable has half-round tops. The cornice carries modillions and has a short return on the gable end. Wood lace crowning the porch repeats something of the three parts displayed in the gable. The iron fence was designed by U. B. Stribling and produced by the firm of Cobb and Stribling. The gate displays the popular lyre design. June Kirk is the present owner.

102. Wright-Holt House

Built in the 1840s with alterations in the 1870s, this house at 416 West Main Street is brick and Italianate, with bracketed cornice, recessed entrance door, and windows which are six over six, except for the windows on the first floor front which are six over nine. The frame stable and carriage house at the rear with arches, lattice, and bargeboard is the finest surviving example in town of this type of architecture. Originally the home of Thomas B. Wright, it belonged later to Samuel Polleys and then to the Vail family. James and Sherrill Holt are the present owners.

Stable and carriage house — *Robert Twente*

Frank S. Baker

Frank S. Baker

103. Francisco-Jordan House

This Italianate brick house at 212 West Second Street was built probably between 1868 and 1874, as the property sold in the latter year for $5,000. The street windows have caps of pressed metal intended to simulate stone and are arched to follow the arch of the windows. These caps, similar to those on other houses in town, could be bought locally from one of several dealers. The somewhat recessed doorway has sidelights and a paneled door with Gothic arches in the top panels. The denticulated cornice over the doorway is supported by corbels. The heavy cornice at the eaves has brackets interspersed with modillions. In the interior the woodwork is painted and artificially grained. Stenciled designs survive on the parlor ceiling.

A one-story high kitchen was attached to the rear of the house. The kitchen had a brick floor, a shed roof with standing seam, and a vent for the stove. Its walls were built of vertical boards toward the alley and open lattice. At the rear of the lot on the alley stands a brick carriage house and stable in good condition. Iron rings for hitching horses are still in the alley wall.

John Coates was the original owner. The house later came into the possession of Hiram Francisco. Fred and Charlotte Jordan now own it.

104. Eckert House

This wedding cake house at 510 West Second Street was built by Madison's first tinsmith, John Eckert. The front facade is made of zinc sheet metal that has been pressed to imitate carved stone. Various designs, such as arched windows and ropes made of pressed metal, indicate the twists and fiber of the sisal plant. A newspaper of April 12, 1872, stated that John Eckert was building "a beautiful little cottage with a galvanized iron front on Second Street between Elm and Vine."[4]

Robert Twente

4. Madison *Daily Evening Star*, 12 April 1872.

John Eckert was listed in the 1867 city directory as a partner in the firm of Braun and Eckert, tinners and gas fitters, at 47 West Main Cross Street. In 1871 he had his own store dealing in stoves and tinware. By 1875 he had joined with Maurice Herbst and expanded business to include stoves, grates, tin, copper, and sheet ironware, to which galvanized iron cornice, slate, and tin roofing were added in 1879. By 1887 the partnership had been dissolved, but Herbst was dealing in galvanized iron cornices. This fact indicates that pressed-metal cornices and window caps were being used to update older houses during the seventies and even in the eighties. The property is now held by Mildred and James Short.

Frank S. Baker

105. Hill-Wolf House

This one-and-a-half-story brick house, built between 1863 and 1870, at 936 West Main Street offers an exuberant example of carpenters' lace. All gable ends and dormers have elaborate decorations at the top that are both cutout and turned. An equally elaborate porch crosses the front and the east side, with the entrance located at the corner at a diagonal. Each of the sidelights at the door is composed of five elliptical glass panes, one above the other. Built for Francis M. and Winnie A. Hill, the house is now owned by Frederick and Berneta Wolf.

106. Marshall-Greiner House

This two-story brick at 809 West Second Street has a bay with four exposed panels located toward the rear on the east side and a heavy Italian bracketed cornice. A recessed doorway, with double doors and highly ornamented colored glass panels set in lead, has an overhanging cap of pressed metal simulating stone supported by brackets. Heavy, elaborate metal caps over the windows are typical of the late Italianate period. The downstairs porch was remodeled with square posts and wood lace when the upstairs porch was enclosed. Chimneys are decorated with panels in the brick, a feature common during the Italianate period. The brick on the front and east facades is hand polished and very smooth, while the west facade is laid up with unpolished brick.

Thomas Bishop obtained the property in 1868 from Addison Marshall for $1,700. This sum indicates that some building existed at that time. Two years later Bishop sold the property for approximately $2,300. The Greiner family owned the property at a later date. It is now in the possession of Anthony and Alice G. Hertz.

Frank S. Baker

107. Friedersdorff House

This three-story brick Italianate apartment building at 512 East Main Street exhibits a style Wilbur Peat describes as "oblong or cubical blocks, usually two stories high and crowned with low-pitched hip roofs and projecting eaves. Brackets, of course, are in evidence, and windows are treated in a variety of ways, more or less faithful to original Renaissance models."[5]

Built probably in 1871–72, this structure displays a low-pitched roof, ornately bracketed cornice, and elaborately shaped window caps with consoles. The windows on the third floor intrude into the cornice. A center portion containing the entranceway projects toward the street and is the full height of the building. The roof of this section extends above that of the main block of the house but follows the same pitch.

The original owner of this magnificent house was Conrad Friedersdorff. C. V. and Sabina Queen are the present owners.

Robert Twente

108. Vail-Holt Building

HABS/HAER

This house at 402 West Main Street was built in 1873 at a cost of $23,000 by Captain Nathan Powell for his daughter, Mrs. W. P. Graham.[6] The large Italianate structure has a wide overhanging cornice supported by brackets, embellished by modillions and dentils, and pierced by windows more horizontal than vertical. Massive bays rise from the ground to cornice. The stone hood molds above the windows are wide and elaborate and varied in design. The window caps on the south face exhibit three different styles. The low-pitched hip roof is surmounted by tall chimneys that show excessive flare at the tops. One of the house's later owners was the Vail family. The owners now are James and Sherrill Holt.

5. Wilbur Peat, *Indiana Houses of the Nineteenth Century* (Indianapolis: Indiana Historical Society, 1962), 124.
6. Madison *Daily Courier*, 10 October 1873.

109. Smith House

Built around 1876, this two-story brick house at 1017 West First Street has a rather heavy Italianate cornice with evenly spaced brackets and slightly arched window caps with keystone decorations. The window caps are pressed metal simulating stone, but the cornice and brackets are of wood. Constructed for Edward and Bridget Smith, the house subsequently belonged to the Moore family and now is owned by Robert L. Smith.

German Collection

Frank S. Baker

110. Stribling House

Because the house at 625 West Second Street was constructed as early as 1837–41, before the appearance of the Italian style in Madison, it must be assumed that its Italianate front was appended considerably later. The irregular roofline seems to indicate successive stages of building, the earliest section being at the back. This story-and-a-half brick house has lateral wings both left and right. The gable toward the front contains a heavily hooded entrance. The second-story central window above the door has a rounded top with shutters of matching shape and is flanked by two porthole windows. A third porthole window is located in the point of the gable. The first-story windows come to the floor and have six over nine panes. The house was built initially for Thomas Vail. Uriah Stribling, famous for his iron fence, owned this house from 1867 to 1900 and erected his patented fence on two sides of the property. The present holders of the property are William and Elizabeth Worthington.

Werner Braun

111. McKim-Miller House

This large, brick, Victorian house at 704 West Second Street was built in 1870 for Robert McKim, coal dealer, furniture manufacturer, and builder. A local tradition has it that he and his partner one day went to the riverfront at flood stage and found a barge of coal floating downstream unattended. They managed to secure it to the bank and obtained certain rights through salvage laws. Suddenly they found themselves in the coal business and on the way toward considerable wealth.

The house, bracketed in a manner reminiscent of the Italianate style and with an Italianate square bay window on the first floor, originally had a three-story observatory in the high Victorian manner extending from the west side and bridged to the second floor of the house. The windows are restrained as is the framing around the entrance. The door is double and filled with decorative glass. Wood skirting that encloses the space below the porch is pierced with openings to supply ventilation and appears to be original. There is still a high Victorian cast-iron fountain on the lawn. A cast-iron deer has disappeared. A later owner of the house was W. A. Barber. Floyd and Susan Miller are the present owners.

112. Schmidt House

This house at 712–14 Walnut Street is a double house, although it is not bilateral. The overwhelming influence of the Italian derived from the Renaissance is evident in this structure. The house has an irregular shape, a small porch in an ell with wood lace of turned posts and spindles, a two-story square tower with a stone band two-thirds of the way up, and a flared roof with gutter and cut-out wood decorations on the cornice. On this small, one-story gabled house is displayed nearly every idiomatic ornament of that period, making the house an amusing example of stylistic exaggeration. It was built between 1861 and 1865 for August Schmidt. Stephen Dugle and Jeanne A. Jurczewski now own it.

German Collection

113. Italianate Double House

This double house at 508 and 510 East Main Street is late Italian, with half-round windows in the right half of the picture and segmental arched windows in the left half. These features probably indicate different dates of construction. The windows with the half-round tops have shutters made to fit. The cornice is the same throughout. The wood lace differs on the porches, possibly indicating different dates of construction. The slate roof carries a colored design in the left half, while the right half is plain. Gertrude Coombs presently owns 508, and Harold Reynolds owns 510.

114. Friedley-Hoffstadt Houses

This double house at 519 and 521 East Main Street, built in 1872–73, shows a continuing cornice and identical window caps on the street facade. The house to the right in the picture lost its doorcap when a late porch was removed. Both houses have interior shutters. The exterior shutters on the house to the left were added by a recent owner. The iron fence was made in Madison by Cobb and Stribling. Initially the house was owned by William Friedley. At present Frank and Margaret Diederich own 519, and Juliet Hoffstadt owns 521. The Hoffstadt family has lived in the house since 1873.

Robert Twente

Frank S. Baker

115. Garrett House

Frank S. Baker

Shingles became relatively prominent as coverings of outside walls, particularly on gable ends, in a late development of the Italian mode during the latter part of the nineteenth century. This style of decoration was not widely used in Madison, but at least one good example can be found, at 207–209 Walnut Street. Shaped shingles cover the gable end on the front facade and form a running band between the first and second levels. All are painted. The apron in the apex of the gable end is unusually elaborate. The windows are two over two with flat casings and lintels. The porch extends across the entire front and has turned posts, a railing with turned balusters, and spindle decorations that are again quite elaborate. Otha and Mary A. Garrett now own the property.

116. 800 Block of Walnut Street

HABS/HAER

815-23 Walnut Street, Federal, 1840s or before

Robert Twente

810 and 812 Walnut Street, probably 1850s
Frank D. Hurdis, Jr.

The 800 block of Walnut Street still retains much of the character of the mid-nineteenth century. Brick houses with entrances directly on the sidewalk, common walls containing chimneys, and no decoration other than brick dentils and smooth lintels indicate construction during the Federal period. Somewhat later, probably in the 1850s, houses such as the two with Italianate porches and bracketed cornices were added. The whole district was so densely populated that the only play areas for children were the streets and the doorsteps.

The row houses have the brick dentils and stone lintels which indicate a date of construction not long after the land was platted in 1842. Walnut Street was one of the early areas of town to be built, and its architectural atmosphere is indicative of that found over much of Madison.

117. Fulton School

Frank S. Baker

The Madison *Daily Courier* of May 20, 1875, contained the following notice:

Mr. B.F. Fowler has been awarded the contract and has commenced work upon the new Fulton school house, on the corner of Second and Ferry streets [now Park and Ferry]. It will be built of brick, one-story high, with galvanized iron cornice, surmounted by a cupola.

At the gable end the roof is supported by paired brackets bearing on the brick wall. Also in the gable end are two entrance doors with transoms that have obviously undergone changes but that may have originally been similar to the windows on the side walls which have caps. These caps project and are supported by corbel-like elements. Original shutters have been removed. The window in the gable end has a heavily projecting round arch.

This school took its name from the little town of Fulton, which was adjacent to Madison to the east. Sometime between 1900 and 1905 the school joined with the Upper Seminary, one of Madison's early public elementary schools. The building is now the property of the Madison Pilgrim Holiness Church.

118. Hunt-Welch Building

This two-story building at 221 East Main Street is one of the oldest buildings on the street. John Hunt initially owned the property on which the structure was erected around 1841. The cornice shows a transition from the Classic mode to the newly developing Italianate style. Damon and Virginia Welch are the present owners.

Frank S. Baker

119. Whitney House

Edwin Whitney obtained this property in 1834 and held it until 1876. Whitney probably built the house at 510 Mulberry Street, and he was the owner when the iron porch was erected in 1854.[7] A picture supplied by Lee Burns shows the house with the iron porch, the Italianate wood cornice, and wood weatherboard siding. In the late 1940s or early 1950s the siding was covered with asbestos shingles. The Burns photograph shows shutters on the upper and lower windows. Now only those on the first floor survive, but they are probably original. The windows in the back are six over six. It may be assumed that the windows in the front were also six over six before they became two over two. The roof is gabled, with one gable facing south and one north. No ornaments appear over the windows, but brackets with pendant finials in the cornices show Italianate influence. The cast-iron porch is very intricate and lacy and is surmounted by an iron balustrade above the roof. The balustrade contains female figures bearing angel wings, four across the front and one at each end. No date or name of supplier appears in the iron porch. The porch floor contains very large dressed stone, as does the sidewalk toward the street. Jonathan and Stephanie Smith are the present owners.

120. Hertz Building

Most of the portion of the alley of the block on the west side of Mulberry between Main and Second streets burned in 1845, and the present buildings are replacements. The building at 317 Mulberry was constructed between 1845 and 1860 in the Italian manner, with Italian decorations over the windows and a heavy Italian cornice pierced with three windows. The decoration around the windows is pressed metal, and the first floor has a cast-iron front.

This building was owned prior to June 18, 1868, by Jacob Smith and may have been the location of his restaurant and saloon. After Smith it was owned by W. and D. Phillips and then by J. Braun. The building served as a shoe store from 1870, when Braun bought it, through the respective ownerships of Peter Denzer and the Hertz family. At the time that the Hertz family sold the building in 1972, a restrictive clause was placed in the deed to protect the facade. The structure is now the property of Darryl and Winnie Smith.

7. Ibid., 11 May 1854.

121. Collins-Davee Building

Tax records indicate that this building at 215 West Main Street was constructed as early as 1825–30.[8] The cornice at the eaves, the hip roof, and the windows on the second floor with their simple lintels reveal an early construction date and the Classic style. The cornice over the door, however, and the cap to the window on the first floor were modified, probably in the sixties or seventies, in the Italian style. The corner entrance is characteristic of Madison architecture in one of its later phases. Other examples of this architectural style occur on the buildings at the corner of Mill and Main, at the corner of Central and Main, at Fourth and Walnut, and on the Broadway Hotel. Other corner entrances have been removed. The original door on this building had a panel of wood which could be put in place at night to protect the glass against intrusion. It was fixed in place by a wood screw about an inch thick. Andrew Collins first owned the property. It belongs now to Thomas Davee.

Werner Braun

122. Zeiser-Harrod Building

The brick dentils, the short second-floor windows, and the flush doorway with sidelights and transom indicate that this business and residential building at 702 West Main Street probably dates between 1835

Frank S. Baker

and 1839. The entrance with sidelights opened into living quarters and stairs. The chamfered entrance, with the ironwork made by the Madison Machine Company, was undoubtedly added at a much later date, possibly as late as 1902. This corner entrance was inserted under and integrated with a stone band that crosses the front and continues on the east wall over the entrance. The plate-glass window is very modern but, judging by the wood panel beneath it, replaces earlier small panes similar to those of the Cisco-Auxier building at 721 West Main. A very good pressed-metal ceiling and, most unusual, pressed-metal sidewalls survive in the store area. Charles Harrod is the present owner.

8. John L. Hopkins, report for the Historic American Buildings Survey no. IN-135, U. S. Department of the Interior, 1.

123. Woodburn-Sparks Iron Front Building

The front of this building at 209 West Main Street, with its iron columns, is similar to the fronts at 324 West Main and 309 Mulberry Street. The iron columns have tall, slim bases and rise in quatrefoil clusters to flaring acanthus leaf capitals, referred to as Tuscan. There are ornamented cast-iron pilasters at the east and west edges of the building. Under the display windows are deeply cut, recessed wooden panels.

The upstairs windows are two over two and have metal caps with consoles and an embellished keystone connecting the raking sides. The metal cornice displays four sets of paired brackets and three equal panels between the sets. The cornice of this building is in many respects similar to that of the building at 324 West Main, a fact that would seem to indicate a single, ingenious designer.

The window caps and cornices are identical with the ones on the building at 213 West Main, which was built in 1853–54 for Davidson and Driggs. These tinsmiths are believed to have furnished the sheet-metal ornaments for their own building and probably supplied those for this building. Richard C. Hubbard initially held this property. Sometime later the Woodburn family owned it. The present owner is Terry Sparks.

Frank S. Baker

124. Iron Front Building

The cast-iron front of this building at 324 West Main Street has quatrefoil columns with flaring capitals decorated with acanthus leaves at the corners, deeply cut panels under the show windows, and sheet-metal cornice across the facade above the first floor. The cornice at the eaves and the caps above the second-story windows are heavily ornamented and of Italianate design. The windows are recent replacements and were originally two over two. Prominent chimneys are bridged in the common wall with the building to the east. The wall to the west rises in a fractable above the roof, which is standing seam metal. The bridged chimneys and the fractable indicate an earlier date of construction for the building than the Italianate additions display. Dennis L. and Mary Anne Harine are the present owners.

German Collection

Frank S. Baker

125. Cisco-Auxier Building

When the Cisco family lived in the rear portion of this building at 721 West Main Street, constructed in 1850 and now attached to the section facing the street, the entrance was the porch decorated with wood lace in the ell of the building. The living quarters were thus separated from the meat market in the front portion of the structure built in 1873 by Charles Quigley. The iron front is almost identical to the fronts on the buildings at 209 and 324 West Main and at 309 Mulberry. They are unsigned, but they must have been made at the same time and most probably by the same manufacturer. The building shows such elements as disengaged iron columns flanking the double doors of the entrance, slightly pedimented stone window caps on the front, bracketed cornice on the front facade only, and hip roof over the front section. The windows in the rear portion have brick segmental lintels. Glass in the show windows and the entrance doors is probably original.

The building was presented to Historic Madison, Inc., by Public Service Indiana in 1964. It was sold with the permission of Public Service Indiana to Margie's Country Store with a preservation clause in the deed. The facade cannot be changed without permission of Historic Madison, Inc.

126. King-Sparks Iron Front Building

HABS/HAER

HABS/HAER

Frank S. Baker

HABS/HAER

This three-story brick at 102-106 East Main Street with heavy, elaborate bracketed cornice represents a somewhat later phase of the Italianate style. The storefront portion of the building comprises one of Madison's best surviving cast-iron fronts. It has four freestanding fluted columns and square fluted pilasters, all with elaborate capitals containing various ornaments: flowers, leaves, scrolls, and egg-and-dart molding. A simply molded cornice extends across the front, above the columns, from pilaster to pilaster. Window sills are stone, but the window caps and the cornice are pressed metal and profusely decorated. The first floor facade on the west portion of the building is a very recent adaptation.

This tall building now has a cornice that is uniform over the complete front. This feature indicates a single owner when the cornice was installed. The back of the building shows that the rear was built as two separate buildings, each with its own roof. At a later date the first floor stores on the Main Street side were handled separately and the present existing iron front was installed on the east half.

Victor and John King acquired the property in 1823 and may have erected a portion of the building which possibly is incorporated in the present structure. Godfrey Dold bought at least a portion of the building in 1862 after a sheriff's sale and is probably responsible for adding the iron front. George Freeman now owns the property at 102, while Julie Sparks owns 104-106.

127. "The Attic"

The land on which these brick storefronts at 629–31 West Main Street are located was transferred from John Paul to James Guthrie in 1829. Over the years the buildings have housed grocery stores, a bakery, and presently a picture-framing shop. There is a carriage house and stable at the rear, and there has always been a residence on the second floor. The iron front was added and bears the date of 1901. The shop windows were originally divided into at least two panes over deeply cut wood panels. The building has a restrained, Italianate cornice and a roof that is metal with standing seams. Catherine Miller was an owner of this property. Philip and Judith George are the present owners.

Frank S. Baker

128. Richert-Cox Building

On the first floor level this three-story brick building at 323–25 East Main Street has three sets of double doors encased in a cast-iron front. The middle set of doors opens directly into a wide staircase to the upper floors. The iron front was made by the Madison Machine Company, which was still flourishing after a

Frank S. Baker

long period of prosperity, and the stone above the entrance identifies the building as the Richert Block, built in 1903. Richert was the name of the owner of a wagon works located somewhere in this block at an earlier date. This front is similar in detail to the ones at "The Attic," 629–31 West Main, installed in 1901, and the Betty Mundt shop at 207 West Main. The prominent cornice is covered with pressed metal, as are the wood panels below the show windows.

The building shows in the cast-iron front and the sheet-metal cornice a strong holdover from a much earlier period when these methods of construction

first became popular. Davidson and Driggs, tinsmiths and stone merchants, are believed to have been installing pressed-metal cornices on the south side of the 200 block of West Main fifty years earlier, in 1853.[9] By the turn of the century manufacturers were making plate glass for show windows in sizes sufficient to fill large spaces. At the present time the property is owned by Richard and Mildred Cox.

129. 200 Block of West Main Street, South Side

The six facades of these commercial buildings at 201–215 West Main Street represent, according to the historian for the Historic American Buildings Survey project in 1978, an assortment of mid-to-late nineteenth-century styles. Most of the fronts, dating

Werner Braun

from the 1830s, started with brick dentils which were later covered with locally produced metal cornices

9. Ibid.

and window caps. These ornamentations may have been added in the 1850s because the designs on the building at 209 West Main Street are exactly the same as those used on the structure at 213 West Main Street, which was built in 1853–54 for Davidson and Driggs. As these metalworkers are believed to have furnished the ornament for the 213 building, they may have created the detailing for the 209 address.[10] Featured in this block are two chamfered corner entrances, each of which employs a single iron column to support the load at the corner. Richard Hubbard was the original owner of these properties.

130. White-Koehler Block

One of the impressive cast-iron facades that has survived in the town is located in the quarter block of 317–27 West Main Street—the Koehler building. It was constructed in different sections, at different dates, with four different cornices. The cast-iron

317-19 West Main   *Frank S. Baker*

323-27 West Main   *Frank S. Baker*

front exhibits round, fluted columns with tall bases, plain flared capitals, and abacus members with concave sides and ornamental molding. Cornices are heavy and bracketed in the Italianate tradition. The second building from the corner of Broadway (House of Flowers) has projecting, slightly pedimented Italianate caps at the windows, while the lintels on the corner building have the smooth surfaces reminiscent of the Classical period.

The brick building next to the alley (liquor store) has six tall arched openings at the street level with keystones. On the second floor are six windows that have curved tops with slightly projecting segmental window caps in brick following the curvature of the windows. The lower edge of the cornice above the windows also is curved to follow the curves of the windows. The whole face is involved in an intricate design which gives the impression of skillful workmanship and an understanding of symmetry and harmony.

Alexander White acquired part of lots 31 and 32 for $600 in 1866. He purchased other portions of these lots, bordering on Broadway, in 1872 for $8,167. This figure indicates that there was substantial building on these portions at that time. White sold some portions of the east property in 1876 for $8,500. This property was probably that part bought in 1866 for $600. Buildings on this end, therefore, were apparently constructed prior to 1876. The Koehler family owns the buildings.

10. Ibid.

131. 100 Block of West Main Street, South Side

HABS/HAER

This group of buildings on the south side of the 100 block of West Main Street has undergone many changes. Facades have changed from Federal to Italianate, and ornaments have been added to the window caps and cornices. Brick dentils have become lost or hidden under cornices of pressed metal. The building at 109 West Main Street (far left in illustrations) had brick dentils at the eaves and six over six windows in the Federal style. Probably built in the 1840s, this structure was completely rebuilt after 1875 in the Italianate manner with the pressed-metal bay.

The tall building to the immediate right, 111 West Main Street, with the modified Palladian roofline, has lost the iron front on the first floor, as shown in the earlier photograph. Upper floors remain unchanged. A prospectus for this building appeared in the Madison *Courier* of July 26, 1867.

In mid 1870s   *HMI*

G. M. BROOKS'S NEW BUSINESS HOUSE. Mr. Gilbert M. Brooks has determined to erect a new palatial building that will be an ornament to the city.... The general design of the house is to be Romanesque. The front of the first story will be of glazed iron, containing two large windows, 11 by 6 feet, filled with single panes of French plate glass, and one large folding door filled with a single pane of plate glass eight feet by two and a half in each fold. The main front will be of brick with free stone dressing and iron window caps, of a new and beautiful design by Connett & Bro., the architects of the entire building. The front will be further ornamented by four large brick pilasters with handsomely cut stone caps. The top of the front will be finished with a heavy bracketed cornice surmounted by an arched center piece, heavily moulded. The second and third stories...with three windows each filled with double thick French glass—four lights to the window, each pane forty-eight by sixteen inches. The windows in the two upper stories will be further embelished [sic] over the iron caps with caison and dentils under the sill. The rooms will be twenty feet wide by eighty-five feet deep in the clear. The staircases leading to the carpet room in the second story, the wholesale room in the basement, and the storing room in the third story, will be of heavy walnut rail — carved newal [sic] post — with handsomely ornamented ash balusters. In the rear part of the carpet room there will be a balustered floor light to admit light from the rear windows of the second story. The entire building will be heated in the winter season by "Loize's Patent Moist Warm Air Furnace," located in the basement.... When completed it will stand near eighteen feet higher than any other business house on Main Cross Street.... We have no hesitation, judging from the design and drawings, in saying that it will be the handsomest business house in the State.

In the next building, 113 West Main Street, the long windows on the upper floor have heavy window caps. The brick dentils were lost when the building was heightened and given an Italianate cornice. The lower floor appears to have been changed from brick to iron to modern glass. This same succession of changes also occurred on the lower floor of the next building, at 115 West Main Street, although upper floors have been altered very little. The building has been heightened, and the Italianate cornice has been lifted and given finials at the corners. The building at the far right was probably changed from an 1840s Federal style, as evidenced in the short windows on the upper floors, to the Italianate style, as seen in the cornice, window caps, and iron front.

132. 100 Block of West Main Street, North Side

Frank S. Baker

The 100 block on the north side of West Main Street gives a good indication of the importance of iron fronts in Madison in the second half of the nineteenth century when owners were competing with each other in updating their storefronts with cast iron. Ellen Sheridan and Hiram Quigley originally owned the properties.

The three-story building at 108 West Main Street (right) has an ornate, metal cornice with heavy brackets. The cornice is strongly Italianate, as are the window caps which are rounded in segmental arches. This building has an iron front and one of the few surviving iron balconies in town. The cast-iron columns flanking the doorway and the pilasters at the corners of the building are square and paneled. The iron cornice under the balcony is ornamented with Classic egg-and-dart molding, and elaborate medallions cover the bolts which attach the cornice to the building. Sales noted on the abstract imply that a building was on this lot in 1867, or at least by 1872.

The Italianate building at 110 West Main Street (center) has quatrefoil cast-iron posts with tall bases and flared capitals with acanthus leaves and square cast-iron paneled pilasters with rosettes at the top. There is a pressed-metal cornice across the front at the head of the first floor and another sheet-metal cornice at the eaves, with single brackets and raised ornaments between. The entire front is covered with ornamental pressed metal, the only survivor of its kind in town. The Preston family presently owns 108 and 110.

The heavily decorated facade of the building at 116 West Main Street (left) has ornamented cast-iron posts with flat sides surmounted by a cast-iron cornice crossing the entire front of the building above the first floor. Iron pilasters occur at the extremes of the facade in the same form as the posts flanking the entrance. The entrance is a single door, deeply recessed within slanted plate-glass windows. A plaque on the ironwork indicates that it was made by George L. Mesker and Company, Ironworks, Evansville, Indiana. The cornice at the eaves is sheet metal with brackets at the corners topped by metal urns. The brick front of the second floor is divided into three panels, each containing a window with graduated brick courses at the top. Lloyd Jones and William Liter now own this building.

133. 200 Block of East Main Street, North Side

HABS/HAER

This group of four buildings at 223–29 East Main Street follows the standard pattern of the Italianate bracketed style in the nineteenth century. In each, the first floor is one long, narrow room used for retail business. The upper floors are open rooms which can be used for storage by the tenants below or for other businesses or offices. These buildings were constructed for Peter Bierck and Otto Heuse as a continuous block of four storefronts. The tax records show an increase in improvement values from $590 in 1880 to $2,780 in 1881. The buildings are highly detailed in ornament, which is composed of sheet-metal cornices and window caps typical of the tastes of Madison at this time. The one first-floor facade which remains in its original condition is that of Wheeler's Barber Shop (second from right). This metal front was made by B. Busch and Sons, Columbus, Ohio. Herschel and John Wheeler own 227, while Madison First Federal Savings and Loan owns 223, 225, and 229.

Werner Braun

134. Niklaus-Scott Block

This block, 301–311 West Main Street, comprises a main building on the west (right), originally owned by John Niklaus, and two smaller sections on the east. Niklaus came to Madison from Switzerland in the 1840s and bought one section of this block soon after his arrival. Presumably the section next to the alley (right) was the earliest but was later changed. A third story was added, and the windows and cornice were made to match the adjoining section. Differences in the pattern of fenestration in three different sections of the building probably indicate different times of construction. The windows of the different sections have heavy caps that are similar but not identical. A heavily decorated cornice with Italianate brackets is located at the eaves and runs the length of the block from Poplar Street to the alley. The date 1884 on the front of the blocks refers to the time that John Niklaus turned the business over to his son, not the date of the building. Several store buildings facing on Main Street at the east (left) end of the block were individually owned until bought by Elmer and John Scott. All but the corner building have had the first floor storefronts modernized with extensive alterations. The Scott family is the present owner.

VII

French Second Empire

THE SECOND EMPIRE style, named for the reign of Napoleon III (1852–70) and popular in America in the 1860s and 1870s, continued the emphasis of the picturesque found in the Gothic Revival and Italianate styles. Soon after the middle of the nineteenth century, according to Wilbur Peat, "American architects became engrossed...[in] what is now generally known as the French Imperial or French Second Empire. It was not a revival in the sense of being a free interpretation of an antique European style, but rather an adoption with relatively minor modifications of a current French movement— a late or baroque stage of Renaissance architecture."[1]

The most distinguishing characteristic of this style is the mansard roof, a form developed by the seventeenth-century architect Francois Mansard and reintroduced into France with the enlargement of the Louvre in 1852–57. The mansard roof is a double-pitched roof with the lower slope steeper than the upper. By increasing head room in the attic, it provided an additional usable floor. To give light to this level, the mansard was almost always pierced with dormers.

Another characteristic of Second Empire architecture is the heavily bracketed cornice introduced beneath the mansard. Brackets are sometimes paired and are other times arranged in long and evenly spaced strings across the facade. In many instances they stretch around the sides and rear of a building as well.

135. Masonic Temple

This building at 217–19 East Main Street was constructed in 1871–72. According to the Historic American Buildings Survey, it "was constructed using many of the standard details of the Second Empire style, including curved window cap pediments, iron crestings, and collunettes. The mansard roof originally was pierced by eight chimneys, and featured cast-iron urns at the corners, with iron cresting atop the roofline. Of special note on the facade of the building are the stone ball and water-leaf capitals of the small collunettes that set off the storefronts of the first floor, which are beautiful examples of the talents of local stone cutters."[2]

As is true of many Second Empire structures, this building is entirely symmetrical. The heavily projecting cornice is supported by a great many brackets which give a rhythmic accent to this crowning decoration to the facade, interrupted only by the central gable with its peak rising above the mansard. The rhythm is continued through the window arrangement and window caps.

John R. Temperly was paid $835 for the plans and specifications of the Masonic Temple. He was born in 1831, the eldest son of Matthew Temperly, ar-

1. Wilbur Peat, *Indiana Houses of the Nineteenth Century* (Indianapolis: Indiana Historical Society, 1962), 129.
2. U. S. Department of the Interior, Historic American Buildings Survey, no. IN-134, 5.

chitect. The building's total cost was $25,132.70. The plan included stores on the first floor, offices on the second, and lodge rooms on the third. Gas pipes were laid in as the building was constructed.

In its Madison Main Street Project, 1977–80, the National Trust for Historic Preservation placed great emphasis on signage. Steinhardt and Hanson, longtime tenant on the first floor, was one of the first businesses to do away with its modern sign and erect one compatible with the old architecture.

Frank S. Baker

136. Bear Building

The French Empire style is manifest in this 1870s building at 206 East Main Street. A mansard roof pierced with six windows shields the third floor.

Robert Twente

These windows are slightly arched, have heavy caps supported by consoles, and are surmounted by an inconspicuous cornice. The upper slope of the roof is not visible from the street, although a fractable wall appears at the east extremity (left). A pair of slender chimneys rises from a middle wall marked by another fractable. A second pair of similar chimneys rises from the west wall (right). Below the mansard a very massive and heavily bracketed cornice extends the width of the building, punctuated by seven unusually large brackets which extend down between the windows of the second floor. Below the cornice are six tall windows with half-round tops and heavy extended caps with keystone-like ornaments in the centers of the arches. Panes in the windows of both the second and third floor are two over two. Those on the second floor are much longer. The cornice between the first and second floor is original and in stone. Iron pilasters at the extremities and again in the middle of the facade are integrated with the first floor cornice. Show windows have recently been rebuilt.

Ascher Hoffstadt owned the property between 1863 and 1881. He lived in the building where he operated a dry goods store. Albert Bach acquired the property in 1891, had a dry goods store at the street level, and lived above prior to his purchase of his big house at 732 West Main Street. Oscar and Norma Bear are the present owners.

137. Mansard Residence

This house at 504 West Second Street is an example of a residence with a mansard roof. It was probably built in the mid-1870s. Built for two families, the structure had three rooms down and three rooms up for each family, each half with its own staircase. Windows on the first floor are two over two. Those on the front have stone lintels, and those on the sides have segmental arches of brick. On the second floor, double dormers in the mansard exhibit an ornamental device in the lintel. A small projecting cornice dividing the side wall from the mansard contains brackets and a frieze of cutout sawtooth design openings done with a scroll saw. The original slate roof has been replaced, and the porch is modern. Robert and Alice Hoffman own the property.

Frank S. Baker

VIII

Queen Anne Revival-Eastlake

IN AMERICA during the decades following the aftermath of the Civil War, architecture in general ceased to be classic and became decidedly eclectic. Of the several picturesque styles which developed during the 1880s and 1890s, probably the most popular were the so-called Queen Anne Revival and the Eastlake.

The Queen Anne mode originated in England where the term was used to describe buildings imitating the architecture of the pre-Georgian period. Its chief proponent was Richard Norman Shaw (1831–1912). The American architect Henry Hobson Richardson (1838–86) introduced it in this country with his design for the 'summer cottage,' the Watts-Sherman house in Newport, Rhode Island, in 1874.

Because the style predated the short reign of Anne, Wilbur Peat preferred the term Neo Jacobean. Marcus Whiffen, calling Queen Anne "an egregious misnomer," thought it might better be called Queen Elizabeth.[1] Other names have been suggested by architectural historians: Free Classic, Modified English, American Vernacular, American Craftsmen, and, probably the one that best describes it, Shavian Manorial, after the designs of Richard Shaw.

The term Eastlake, named for the English architect and furniture designer Charles Locke Eastlake (1833–1906), might also be considered a misnomer. Eastlake himself decried the use of his name to identify a style with which he had "no real sympathy."[2]

Despite the controversy and clamor over nomenclature, the names Queen Anne and Eastlake have persisted to the present. Essentially the styles are similar except that many of the decorative details of the latter have been borrowed from Eastlake's own furniture designs.

The typical domestic structure in America had its antecedents in the early English cottages, but through the many additions and alterations made through the years, the styles of these structures became far removed from the original prototypes. Distinguishing characteristics are irregularity of mass or plan, diversity of materials, and variety of color and texture. Architectural embellishments include high and multiple roofs, elaborate chimneys paneled or modeled in brick or stone, gables, curved brackets, balconies, porches, bay windows, and turrets with conical roofs. Decorative elements were made by lathe, scroll saw, and chisel.

In Madison few houses were built in the Queen Anne or Eastlake mode, but those extant illustrate many of the characteristics mentioned above.

---

1. Marcus Whiffen, *American Architecture Since 1780: A Guide to the Styles* (Cambridge, Mass.: M.I.T. Press, 1969), 115.
2. Ibid., 124.

Frank S. Baker

138. Trow House

This house at 512 West Street, directly north of the Second Presbyterian Church (now Historic Madison's Auditorium) and built between 1878 and 1881, possesses almost all of the elements of the Queen Anne-Eastlake style, both in materials and design. These elements include bricks, stone, shingles, weatherboarding, sharply pointed dormer gables with scroll saw cutout patterns and extended hoods, bays, stained glass, and decorative ironwork. Paint on the exterior woodwork was applied at the time the house was built; paint on the bricks was added in the 1970s. A large fireplace chimney is pierced by a window containing stained glass laced with unusually thin lead strips.

The deed records show that the property was owned prior to November 21, 1877, by James W. Hinds and sold on that date to Eva Trow for $700. It was sold June 5, 1879, for $2,250 by William Trow, Sr., to William Trow, Jr. In 1881 the widow of the latter, Susan M. Trow, sold the property for $4,100 to Louis L. Powell. The house was probably complete by that date. Anthony Dattilo later owned the house. The present owner is Madison First Federal Savings and Loan Association.

139. Gibson-Yunker House

Another example of the Queen Anne-Eastlake style is this house at 1050 Michigan Road. Located on the hill above the city, the house was built in 1871–72 by Aurelius Gibson from the designs of his Boston architect, George D. Rand. It contains many different materials, including hard-pressed brick, stone,

Frank S. Baker

slate, tile, and turned, carved, and scroll-sawed wood. Steep gables are ornamented with triangular aprons of thin wood at their peaks, and these are decorated with cutouts by scroll saws. A turret with a conical roof and tall, elaborate chimneys are other features of the house. In 1949 the living room was enlarged, and a picture window and terraces were added. The materials used in the interior vary to such an extent that the woodwork differs in each room. Oak, walnut, cherry, and butternut woods are used. Thomas and Barbara Hearn now own the house.

140. Kirk-Denton House

Frank S. Baker

This house at 514 East Main Street was built about 1890 and illustrates some of the picturesque qualities of the late Queen Anne-Eastlake style. The restless contour of this building results from its asymmetrical massing. Also characteristic is the combination of sharp gables, beveled corners, windows on the front projection with their ornamented hoods, iron lace on the comb of the roof and on the cutaway corner projections, stained glass, filigreed hardware, shingles, a porch with wood lace, and tall, rather elaborate chimneys. The highly stylized sunburst design within the gable of the main entrance is especially typical of Eastlake ornamentation. William Kirk initially owned the property. The present owners are Howard and Grace Denton.

IX

Mixed Styles

AS INDICATED previously, most of the buildings in Madison show a considerable mixture of architectural styles. Some, however, are so extensively mixed that they warrant special treatment in this section. Modifications after construction have in many instances almost wholly obliterated earlier stylistic elements. In other instances different styles were included in the original design. The mixture of styles as demonstrated by the houses in this group varies, with no two buildings showing the same mix.

141. Kestner House

This bank house, built on a hillside at 620 Spring Street, is unlike any other house in Madison in that it shows Dutch derivation. The gambrel roof is not usual in this part of the country. Found frequently in the early houses in eastern Pennsylvania, the stylistic elements may have been brought to Madison by one of the early German families from that area.

Other elements are interesting, although impossible to classify under any particular style. The outside staircase to the second level originally approached from the west and led to the second floor porch. It has been altered in recent years to enter the front room instead of the porch. Windows are nine over six, six over six, and two over two. The walls of the first floor are stone, and those of the second floor are brick. Windows have stone lintels, except for two in the gable. The original brick floor which was laid in very interesting designs has been replaced by a simpler one.

Tradition has it that John Kestner built the house, and records show he acquired the property in 1853. Richard and Pamela Jones are the present owners.

Robert Twente

Robert Twente

142. Garber-Cassidy Building

Col. Michael Christian Garber bought the Madison *Courier* in 1849 and probably built the house at 117 West Second Street immediately thereafter. The extreme simplicity of the structure, with its very narrow cornice and brick dentils, looks backward to early nineteenth-century Federal influences. The undecorated window caps, smooth and flush, echo the Classic. The house is presently known as the Luke Apartments, and Bernard and Clorin Cassidy now own the property.

143. Gillett-Schwab House

This house at 517 West Street has many Classic characteristics, including smooth stone lintels, a low gable, and a considerably recessed doorway surmounted by a Classic cornice. A cornice at the eaves is basically Classic but became Composite by the addition of interspaced brackets in the original design. The ironwork at the entrance included the lyre design on one side and a railing with an endpost surmounted by a Sheffield silver ball on the other. This railing has since disappeared. Built for Simeon Gillett between 1846 and 1856, the house was later owned by George Schwab and later still by Lyle and Charlotte Peterson. King's Daughters' Hospital now owns the building.

Frank S. Baker

144. Hites-Good House

On the site of this house at 1034 Michigan Road there was a tanyard owned by a man named Hites and built probably as early as 1811. The original foundations of its early buildings survive in the

Frank S. Baker

present house, built around the 1830s. The style of the house is mixed, with elements surviving from the Federal, Classic, and Italianate periods. Windows are six over six, and many of the panes are original imperfect glass. The ironwork on the porches is a much later addition.

A fine spring which emerged from the hillside near the road was known as Cornett Spring and was used for many years by travelers up and down the Michigan Road. Thomas and Virginia Good are the present owners of the house.

145. Madison Country Club

A farmhouse at the west end of Main Street, now the Madison Country Club, was originally a plain, simple brick Federal structure, characteristic of many farmhouses of the early nineteenth century. It has

Frank S. Baker

undergone many alterations, each time with the addition of ornaments, such as Italianate cornices. The diligent searcher can discover the original front entrance, which faced the river and now forms a doorway between two dining rooms. This doorway still has the original sidelights.

The house, situated on a forty-five-acre tract, was built by J.W. Hunter, probably soon after he bought the property in 1841. It was the base of a major Civil War hospital. From 1901 to 1929 the building was used by the Madison Chautauqua Association. This organization also had a barn-like structure toward the river which could hold a large number of people.

146. Thomas-Cassidy House

Built probably between 1833 and 1839 with successive alterations, this house at 605 West Second Street is an example of continued adjustment to new fashions, including the addition of brackets in the cornice, a portico, and a recent autoport. The stucco may be original, since it was popular in Madison at least as early as 1835, when it was used by Edwin J. Peck on the exterior walls of Historic Madison's Auditorium. Thomas Thomas first owned the property. Harold and Kathryn Cassidy are the present owners.

Steve White

Frank S. Baker

147. Cosby-Barber Building

This building at 407 East Main Street, originally owned by Archibald Cosby, followed the Federal style characteristic of the 1830s in Madison. According to Tri-Kappa's *Tour of Historic Homes,* "It was modified in the late nineteenth century by the addition of window caps, an oval transom above the front door and metal ornaments under the eaves of the gable facing the street."[1] Thus the building illustrates the merging of two different styles. Dr. G. Hewitt was allowed in 1890 to close a passage between his office and the fire station next door, adding those few feet to the interior of his building and making the firehouse wall a common one. The present owner is Frances Talkington.

1. Tri-Kappa, *Tour of Historic Homes,* 1976.

Frank S. Baker

148. Drusilla Building

This building at 601 Broadway has been subjected to many alterations and is now composite in style. The original building was erected by James Johnson between 1834 and 1841, probably in the Federal style. The first addition, which faced south, was made by William Wells during the Civil War and doubled its size. It made the house cubic and Classic in form. In 1903 Miss Drusilla Cravens, the granddaughter of James F. D. Lanier, enlarged the building with an addition to the east and converted it to a residence for elderly ladies. This addition included the entrance doorway to the east, with fanlight and sidelights and the Palladian window on the second floor. Also at this time the portico was added with the fluted columns and Ionic capitals. At some time, probably when the

east addition was built, an Italianate cornice was added. Windows occur in different sizes and shapes but appear to have been six over six in the early stages of the building. Those in the east addition were, and still are, six over nine on the first floor. Probably at this time other windows on the south face were extended to the floor. The hip roof is in the Classic manner and is nearly invisible from the street.

A third addition was made to the west in 1982 when the building was converted for the use of a medical clinic. At this time the Italianate cornice was extended to encircle the new portion, and a new door was added on the south face of the addition. The heavy columns with the lotus capitals at the south entrance came from the Madison Hotel, which was demolished in 1948. The Drusilla Professional Group is the present owner.

149. Alling-Naill House

The original part of this house at 521 Jefferson Street was built before 1828 by Richard C. Talbott and is Federal in style. Purchased by John Alling in 1828, it became known as the Alling homestead and remained in the family until 1903. A staircase and part of the second floor were added during the Civil War. The kitchen, dining room, and the second-floor room over the dining room were added later. The Classic porch was not built until the twentieth century. John Naill subsequently held title to the property. At present the owners are Steven and Linda Conarroe.

Frank S. Baker

150. Cravens House

This brick house at 122 Fairmount Drive, when built for H. F. Swope in 1885, followed the T-shape popularized in the Italianate revival. It has a two-story Greek portico that was added by Miss Drusilla Cravens about 1903. Brick for the house was fired in Madison, and all the walls between the rooms are of two layers of brick with an insulation space between. The porch was destroyed in the tornado of 1974, and the columns were replaced by the same firm in Pittsburgh which supplied the original columns. Thomas and Lynda Breitweiser are the present owners.

Robert Twente

Robert Twente

151. Wilbur-Reindollar House

This house at 226 Maywood Lane, owned and probably built by Shadrack Wilbur in the early 1830s, has undergone many changes. Originally a one-and-a-half-story farmhouse, in later years, probably during the Second Empire period, a mansard roof was added. In 1925 this roof was removed and replaced by the present roof when Drusilla Cravens added the front portico and columns. The long galleries at the rear of the house, showing a strong southern influence, are said to be original. There were six cisterns on the property. One was used for drinking water and had a brick wall across the middle. The water from the roof would enter the cistern on the one side of the wall, filter through the bricks, and then be pumped for drinking. The small brick building across the driveway at the west side of the house,

known as Caesar's cottage, contained a root cellar. The small detached house at the east side, known as Brutus's cottage, was at one time used by the help. Other outbuildings include barns, a carriage house, and stables. The site was known as Wilbur's Point and still offers fine views of the river. Besides Wilbur and Cravens, holders of the property have included Bushrod Taylor and George and Mildred May. Vernay and Dorothy Reindollar now own it.

X

Stone Buildings

THERE ARE SEVERAL stone buildings in Madison which survived in fine condition. Stone was available as a building material from various sources. The town is surrounded by hills of limestone, and numerous small quarries sprang up very early on the hillsides, where dressed stone was produced for houses, for quoins, and for door framings in houses and barns. More readily available stone was in the creek beds, where torrents of water flowed rapidly when it rained and ran off to leave dry stones at other times. These stones, subject to freezing in the winter, broke into usable sizes and were easily handled. They frequently came away in straight, smooth blocks and could be tapped with a hammer to make beautiful corners, square right angles, flat tops and bottoms, and square sides.

All of this available stone resulted in the building of great barns, a number of which were livery stables. The old directories and newspapers indicate there must have been at least one livery stable on every block. Some of the barns that remain have a whole row of little horse windows large enough for a horse to put his head through and to get some idea of daylight outside. One such livery stable on Broadway between Second and Main Cross, no longer in existence, had fifty horses to rent and boarded many others.

Frank S. Baker

152. Christman Barn

George and Theresa Christman migrated from Germany to Pennsylvania and then to Madison, Indiana, where their youngest son, John, was born in 1859. Prior to 1859 they built a stone barn covered with stucco beside a free-flowing spring where they established a dairy. The barn at 633 Spring Street has a hip roof with standing seams, a style which is most unusual for barns in this area. The spring was used for cooling milk and has a flow even today five or six inches in diameter. Some of the original Dutch doors remain today, but others have been replaced. Horses were kept in the ell to the right in the picture. Adam Christman is the present owner.

Frank S. Baker

153. Old Icehouse

Tradition has it that this building on the west side of Walnut Street between Second and First streets was originally an icehouse, and its construction bears out that identification. The walls of undressed stone, probably gathered from streambeds, are two feet or more thick, and the floor now at ground level has been constructed to cover a pit which is now the basement. The only openings in the outside walls were two windows high in the gables near the peak of the roof used for admitting ice. Various openings have been cut in the walls in recent years.

The building is forty by sixty-eight feet with a two-pitch roof. It has east and west gable ends rising thirty feet above the street level, and eaves fifteen feet above ground level. This building provided a very large area for the storage of ice. The building is the property of Richard T. Heck.

154. Meyers Stone Barn

This large stone barn on East First Street between Jefferson and Walnut streets has undergone many alterations. Various original openings, now closed, indicate the presence of a hay door on the second level and small horse windows on the first level. This evidence gives credibility to the tradition that the building was at one time a stable and carriage house. Around the beginning of this century, it became an abattoir or slaughterhouse. Meyers and Son Manufacturing Company owns the barn.

Frank S. Baker

155. City Livery Stable

This long building on Third and Fourth streets on the alley between Jefferson and Mulberry was a livery stable with horse doors on the first level and hay doors on the second level. The corner at the alley intersection is chamfered with a wagon door on the first level and a large hay door above. A metal roof extends over the chamfered hay door, and small horse windows appear in a row on the alley side. This building has been called the City Livery Stable. Whether this title indicates municipal ownership, or is only a name, is unknown. The present owners are Wallace and Norma Ferguson.

Frank S. Baker

XI

Railway Station

IN COMMUNITIES across the United States the railway station designated economic and social progress. During the formative years of railway construction, railroad companies gave slight consideration to architectural fashion in designing terminals, choosing instead a rather simple utilitarian style. The subsequent development of more elaborate passenger service, with an eye to comfort, especially in passenger cars, generated the building of grand impressive stations. Madison's 1890s octagon station is a remarkable structure primarily because its shape is almost exclusively seen in barns or residences, not

HABS/HAER

in public or commercial buildings. Most popular at mid-century, the octagon form never achieved the esteem that, to some supporters, its aesthetic and functional qualities merited.

156. Railway Station

The railroad station at 615 West First Street is the second passenger railroad station to be built in Madison. It is Madison's only example of the octagon style. The land was acquired from Alexander C. Lanier and Silas Howe in 1893, and the station was constructed in 1895 for the Pittsburgh, Cincinnati, Chicago, and St. Louis Railroad Company. The contractor for the building was a Mr. Drury of Richmond, Indiana.

A bronze bell was hung from a tripod close to the ground and was struck by hand with a hammer an hour before the time of departure of the train. Although the building was last used as a passenger station in 1935, ownership was retained by the Pennsylvania Railroad until the early 1960s.

The station of sandstone and buff brick originally included the octagonal section, used as the passenger waiting room, and an extension to the west which contained the baggage area and the ticket office. A three-window bay facing the track allowed observation of the movement of trains in either direction. The upper part of the octagon appears as a cupola above the porch roof and contains clerestory windows which admitted light to the waiting room below. Originally the clerestory was fitted with leaded stained glass, the roof was slate, and the porch completely encircled the building. The porch roof is supported by wood columns, turned in the middle with square sections at the ends. The columns are

attached to the roof of the porch by triangular brackets with cutout areas and are characteristic of many of the porch posts of the period. The floor of the porch was a brick pavement which extended to the street and along the track both east and west. Most of this brick paving remains.

The waiting room was plastered below the clerestory but had a high wainscot of beaded and paneled wood around the perimeter. The ceiling of the octagon is coffered, and the upper part of the walls, now within an upstairs room, contains panels with pilasters at the corners of the octagon and a cornice with moldings around the upper edge. The double entrance doors to the waiting room are paneled and carved and contain oval, beveled glass. The ticket window within the waiting room has a pane of rippled glass with the word "Tickets" molded in the glass.

A stenciled design, a logo-like emblem of the Pennsylvania Railroad that was painted in a border slightly below the ceiling of the baggage and ticket areas, has been preserved. The same decoration may have been used in the waiting room, but if so, it has been covered with paint. Bernard and Esther Wilson are the present owners of the old station.

XII

Firehouses

IT IS DIFFICULT for people today to realize the important role that the fire companies played in the lives of early communities. In Madison this role may be better understood because here volunteer fire companies still exist and flourish. Firehouses were the social centers of the town, and it was necessary for them to have special extensions to accommodate this usage. Architecture was not only functional but also highly stylized and fully decorative.

157. Fair Play Fire Company No. 1

Firehouse No. 1 at 403 East Main Street is Italianate in style, with a tower that derives from those that were all over Italy in the Middle Ages, especially in the Tuscan and Lombard regions. The tower's upper courses of brick, which originally flared out, were removed a few years ago when they were found to be dangerously unstable. The tower is not, therefore, as true to type as it was originally. Atop this tower is a figure of a fireman forming a weathervane. This figure is affectionately called "Little Jimmy." The original "Jimmy" was provided by John Adams's metalsmithing shop for $28.85. The original building was erected probably in 1875 by the Madison Street Railway Company as a trolley barn. James White was the architect. It was sold for $8,000 in 1888 to the Fair Play Company, which built the tower and made other alterations. Three horse stalls were added, and

Frank S. Baker

the names of the horses painted above the doors can still be seen. One of the old fire wagons is still on view. The record books of the fire company, organized in 1841, have been preserved and are an invaluable source in tracing various items of historical interest. The building was one of the most important social centers in the town. Dinners were served from the kitchen at the rear.

According to the Historic American Buildings Survey history of this building, the company decided in 1896 "to lay brick on the sidewalks around the property.... The brick was purchased from the Nelsonville (OH) Sewer Pipe Company for $61.66. The brick that was laid is partly still in place to the front of the engine house and was called the 'star pattern.' The design of this brick...has been selected by the National Trust for Historical Preservation for the logo design of its Main Street Project, working on the preservation of business districts in smaller American cities."[1]

Robert Twente

158. Washington Fire Company No. 2

This building at 104 West Third Street is designed in the Classic manner. Built in 1848–49, it is believed to be the oldest firehouse in continuous use in Indiana. It is a long, rectangular, brick building on a stone foundation, with pedimented gable end facing the street. Surviving windows are six over six. The engine door, which has been extensively enlarged for modern equipment, was originally arched with brick, and the line of the original arch remains visible today. Windows in the front facade have smooth undecorated stone lintels and stone sills. The cornice on the

1. U.S. Department of the Interior, *Historic American Buildings Survey*, no. IN-90.

H. M. Flora

were removed to the Lanier house many years ago where they still hang in the parlors. The Washington Fire Company was known as the "Silk Stocking Company" because of the wealth of many of its members, two of whom were Shrewsbury and Lanier.

Since Temperly and Dutton, architects of the firehouse, used the same design in the capitals of their columns as Costigan used in the drawing room of the Shrewsbury house and on the portico of the Lanier house, it seems obvious that both Costigan and Matthew Temperly had access to a copy of Lafever's carpenter's handbook of 1835.[2]

sides is corbeled brick. A boxed, wooden, horizontal cornice on the front gable returns on each side.

This firehouse was also a social center. A large room on the second floor was used as a ballroom for dinners and for public gatherings. A colonnaded screen at one end of the room marked off an area for a speaker or for amateur theatricals. The screen contains two fluted columns with lotus blossom capitals and garland design on the abacus. The architrave has tongue-and-dart molding and the painted frieze has "Washington Fire Co. No. 2" in the corner section, with "Organized January 20, 1846" on one side and "Incorporated January 15, 1849" on the other. At the boxed cornice are dentils. A half-pilaster is at each side, and a simple cornice molding encircles the room. Two rectangular plaster ceiling panels contain bead and reel, water leaf, and egg-and-dart moldings and flowers that match those on the capitals. The crystal chandeliers which hung from these panels were purchased in Austria. They

2. Minard LaFever, *The Beauties of Modern Architecture*, vol. 18 of *Da Capo Press Series in Architecture and Decorative Art* (1835; reprint Da Capo Press, 1968), plate 11.

159. Walnut Street Fire Company No. 4

Mayor Alexander White designed and presumably built this brick Italianate fire station at 808 Walnut Street in 1874. It had one room on the first floor and one room on the second. The facade contained a large working door for the fire engine and two side doors, all three doorways surmounted by circular arched tops. The construction cost of the entire building was approximately $1,900, with $221 in addition for the bell for the tower, which was destroyed in 1933. The bell was moved to a new steel tower at the rear of the building and in 1961 was installed in the new fire station at Third and Walnut.

According to the fire company minute books, in 1893 the facade was replaced with an iron front. At the same time the arches were removed, and the openings became square. The ironwork was planned by James White, a nephew of the original builder, and installed by John Forsee, who was paid $448 for this new iron front. At the time Hoffman and Quinn were paid $79.40 for a galvanized cornice, and a bull's eye window was purchased from the City Planning Mill for $7.00. In 1887 a fire cistern was installed behind the engine house.

After the fire engine company moved to a new building in 1961, this building became the headquarters of the county Republican organization.

HABS/HAER

Industrial Architecture

INDUSTRIAL ARCHITECTURE in the nineteenth century as illustrated by examples found in Madison was essentially functional rather than stylized, with little or no ornamentation. When ornamentation appeared it reflected the style expressed in houses of the time, e.g., Classic, Gothic, Italianate, etc. Major influences were the need for the proper amount of space, strength in floors and walls, light, ceiling heights adequate to acccommodate belts, belt wheels and shafts to relay power and distribute it to the proper areas of the building, sources of power, reduced fire hazards, fire control, and proper roofs.

Of these various needs the dominant one was for light. In the effort to admit all possible daylight, great architectural changes were made in fenestration. Artificial gas did not come to Madison until 1851. The gas mantle was not invented until 1884, and before that date gas produced only a flicker, comparable to today's cigarette lighter. The progress in the designing of windows has been indicated in the write-up of each building, from the small early windows to later entire walls of glass. When skylights came into use, they had their architectural effect since they provided light for one floor only. The result was the standard two floor height, with steam engines and electric generator on the lower level and workshops on the naturally lighted upper level. The wall of glass created a taller building but by the same token a somewhat narrower one.

HABS/HAER

160. Madison Gasworks

The structure at First and Walnut streets, built by the Madison Gas-Light Company, was the first gas plant in the Northwest Territory. A Mr. Lockwood of Cincinnati, a noted builder of gasworks in Ohio and Indiana, constructed the plant. The long brick building was designed with four bays each with a gable end facing First Street. Three of these bays have windows six over six in addition to a round ventilator in the gable end. The fourth bay, farthest east, has two carriage doors, one with a stone lintel and one with a brick arch. Brick pilasters at the corners and between the windows make panels.

The interior contained three coke ovens in which coal was baked to drive off gas. When these were no longer used and the machinery was being dismantled, it is said that Henry Ford purchased one of the ovens for his museum of Greenfield Village.

Frank S. Baker

Frank S. Baker

161. Greiner-Mayflower Building

This large main brick building at 928 Park Avenue, originally a brewery and now housing a transfer and storage company, includes an impressive four-story tower with a high hip roof. The main building is topped by a brick cornice with dentils. Windows on the second floor, which appear to be original, are six over six; others have been updated and are now one over one. Windows on the third floor are horizontal, with three narrow vertical panes each. On the first floor windows have been altered with large panes of glass in the show-window manner. Lintels are slightly pedimented.

The two one-story buildings to the east of the main building housed labor for the adjoining brewery. They are Classic in style and constructed of brick with brick dentils in the cornices. One house is a double. The other has the Classic sidelights at the entrance door, with transom over the top. These cottages were probably erected in the 1830s.

In 1854 the local newspaper announced plans for the erection of a large brewery at the east end of town where Second Street meets Sering and becomes Park. It was being built by Mat. Greiner of Cincinnati. In the October 31, 1884, special edition of the Madison *Daily Courier* it was stated that the Madison Brewing Company was organized in August, 1881, and had "since erected buildings thoroughly adapted…. The main brewing building is 40 x 40, 4 stories and occupies the site of the old one…." This old building is the M. Greiner and Sons Brewery. The above description apparently refers to the tower. The three-story building is probably of a somewhat earlier date. On the 1887 map published by J. Niklaus, two towers appear at this location.

162. Trolley Barn

This large, brick building at 717 West Main Street was a market when built in 1875. Afterwards it was owned successively by the Madison Light Company, Madison Light and Railway, and Madison Light and Power. (See the discussion of market houses in chapter 1.) The arched openings on the street side, which admitted the trolley cars, have recently been restored, and the building now houses a number of small shops. The roof is of moderate pitch, with a gable end toward the street and no ornamentation.

Frank S. Baker

163. Miller-Meyers Building

German Collection

Built for Jacob Barnhardt Miller in 1871–72 for a wagon manufacturing establishment at a cost of $1,000, this Italianate brick building at 805–809 Walnut Street has six Roman arches, with windows shaped to fit, on the street facade. On the second floor are six pairs of double-hung windows surmounted by segmental arches in brick. The many windows indicate the need for as much daylight as possible because of the lack of good artificial light. The cornice is heavily bracketed. The building is now used by the Meyers Manufacturing Company as a cutting room. The present owners are Don and Ditten Meyers.

164. Schofield-Meyers Building

The Madison *Daily Evening Star* of April 16, 1877, announced that Alexander White was to build a woolen mill on the northeast corner of High and Main (now First and Jefferson) for J. Schofield and Son, which was moving its business from Vevay. The article mentioned that the building was to have seventy-five windows, emphasizing the need for outside light in a factory at a time when there was very little artificial light available. Until the invention of the gas mantle in 1884, gaslight was only a flicker. It was not until the construction of the Eagle Cotton Mill that windows took over an entire outside wall. The Schofield-Meyers building originally extended on an east-west axis in order to get maximum exposure to the south and a maximum amount of light. Its windows have segmental arches. The gable end facing west displays window caps in the Italianate manner, and the extension to the north has brackets in the same style. The north section may well have been a later addition. The building has housed the Meyers and Son Manufacturing Company since 1937.

Frank S. Baker

165. Schroeder Saddletree Factory

This factory, located north of Milton Street on the west bank of Crooked Creek, is a complex of nineteenth-century industrial buildings which were constructed to house an internationally known company engaged in the manufacturing and distribution

Frank S. Baker

of the wooden forms that support the surface leatherwork on horse saddles. The complex includes a seven-room residence which housed the members of the Schroeder family who worked in the factory, a large workshop building with additions which accommodated a boiler room and power generating shed, a sawmill, a glue shop, a paint shop, a forge, and three outbuildings used for storage. The power plant held a boiler and steam engine, a very early Primm diesel, and Madison's first electric generator. The latter supplied the buildings with electricity. It produced more than needed for the factory so a few neighbor-

HABS/HAER

ing buildings were wired to receive the power. This was Madison's first electric light plant. The Schroeder brothers performed every duty in the production of saddletrees. They went to the woods in winter and cut the trees, put them through the sawmill, stacked and cured the lumber, and saw the process through to the finished product.

John Benedict Schroeder was born in 1844 and came to Madison in the early 1870s. In 1878 he purchased the site of the house and shop buildings from Ann Paul Hendricks for $225. Schroeder probably constructed the original house and shop shortly after purchasing the land. The house with storeroom behind it and the boiler room are made of brick. Other buildings are made of wood. The large wood building on the west shows early repairs of deeply corrugated sheet iron. Windows on the front of the house have stone lintels. Those at the rear have brick segmental arches, a feature that appears in many industrial buildings of the period in Madison. The gable end, facing the street, is elaborately decorated at the apex with a carved and cutout pattern which was popular in the town at that time.

After Ben Schroeder's death in 1908 the family continued the business and incorporated on June 18, 1919, under the name of "Ben Schroeder Company." It remained in operation until the death of Joseph Schroeder in 1972. It was acquired by Historic Madison, Inc., on December 5, 1974, by gift from the Joe Schroeder Trust.[1]

166. Eagle Cotton Mill

HABS/HAER

The Eagle Cotton Mill, at 108 St. Michael's Avenue, was built on the city's gravel bank by the Pittsburgh company of the same name, which moved its manufacturing business to Madison in order to utilize less expensive labor. In the prospectus of the company which appeared in the Madison *Daily Courier* of November 15, 1883, the company was described as a maker of sheeting and seamless bags. In the 1912 city

1. President's Report on the Progress of Historic Madison, Inc., presented at the annual meeting, March 26, 1975.

directory it was listed as making cotton cloths and cordage. The mill was continuously in business until World War II, but in 1942 Meese, Inc., was also listed as using the building.

Robert H. Rankin and James White are credited with having built the mill. This four-story brick and glass building, with one hundred double-hung windows in the wall facing the river, is built with massive wood beams and posts that carry hardwood floors five-and-one-half inches thick. Old Cotton Mill, Inc., is the present owner of the building.

167. Tower Manufacturing Corporation

This factory building at 1001 West Second Street was built in the late nineteenth-century industrial style. According to the cornerstone, it was "erected by R. Johnson & Sons 1884." The first floor facing the river is of undressed stone; the upper story is brick. Skylights were used for illumination and ventilation. The roof is metal and standing seam mounted on a subroof of hardwood four inches thick. Sills under the floor are four inches wide, fourteen inches deep, and placed on ten-inch centers. The basement housed a steam engine which distributed power by belts and shafts and a generator which produced electricity. Robertson, Inc., now owns the property.

Frank S. Baker

Frank S. Baker

168. HMI Warehouse

This lot at 104 Elm Street was sold to Alexander Lanier in 1891, and the building was probably erected by him shortly thereafter. Lanier bought the lot across the alley to the north at the same time and erected on it his carriage house and stable in the same architectural style. In 1902 Drusilla Cravens paid $8,000 for two lots on the east side of Elm Street in the first block north of the river. Judging by the price she paid, the two buildings now on those lots must have been there at that time. The architectural style of the buildings indicates that they could easily have been built between 1890 and 1900. By tradition the building on the lower lot was early used by W. Trow as a cooperage, where barrels were made for shipping the products of Trow's Flour Mill. It served as a livery stable and later was used by Hughes Tobacco Company as a prizing house for grading and packing fine tobacco. The machinery for this packing activity is still intact in the building.

The design of the architecture is very plain, but to some extent Italianate. The gable end facing the street shows Italianate brackets at the cornice that are sturdy and evenly spaced the full length of the cornice. Window caps throughout are slightly arched and outlined with a brick course, giving the impression of caps and corbels found around town in pressed metal. The double window in the gable end and the large double door below it at street level have ornamented wood lintels. These have superimposed cutout decorations somewhat reminiscent of bargeboard designs. Windows are numerous and large, and a number of skylights pierce the roof. The portion of the building facing the street has a floor level high enough from the ground to match the level of a wagon bed for easy loading and unloading of cargo. It also has a second floor supported by massive wooden beams to bear heavy loads, and a deep basement. The building, which extends nearly the full length of the block, has the original slate roof covering a portion of it. Historic Madison, Inc., is the present owner.

German Collection

MOUNTING BLOCK

*T*he mounting block was as common in the nineteenth century as was the horse that the block assisted the rider to mount. It was a single block of stone, usually comprised of three steps. Every household that kept a riding horse had a mounting block, frequently called an "upping block." Today, three survive in Madison.

Glossary

abacus — the uppermost member of the capital of a column; often a plain square slab, but sometimes molded or otherwise enriched.

acanthus — a common plant of the Mediterranean, whose leaves, stylized, form the characteristic decoration of capitals of Corinthian and Composite orders. In scroll form it appears on friezes, panels, etc.

acroterion, akroterion — in classical architecture, one of the angles of a pediment; also, the ornament placed at one of these, especially at the apex.

anta — a pier in classic architecture formed at the termination of a wall and treated as a pilaster, with capital and base.

anthemion — a classic floral running ornament, thought to have been derived from the Greek honeysuckle.

architrave — the lower division of the entablature resting directly upon the columns of a similar group of moldings used to enframe an opening, as a door or window.

balloon frame, balloon framing — a system of framing a wooden building; all vertical structural elements of the exterior bearing walls and partitions consist of single studs which extend the full height of the frame, from the top of the soleplate to the roof plate; all floor joists are fastened by nails to studs.

bargeboard — a board which hangs from the projecting end of a roof covering the gables, often carved and ornamented.

batter — the receding upward slope of a wall or structure.

bead and reel molding — a semiround convex molding decorated with a pattern of disks alternating with round or elongated beads.

belt course — a narrow horizontal band projecting from the exterior walls of a building, usually defining the interior floor levels.

bracket — a support element under eaves, shelves, or other overhangs; often more decorative than functional.

buttress — a projecting structure of masonry or wood for supporting or giving stability to a wall or building.

caisson — a sunken panel, especially in a vaulted ceiling or the inside of a cupola; a coffer.

camelback roof — a single-pitch roof which rises to a peak at one extreme at right angles to the main block of the building, instead of a peak in the middle as is the case of a two-pitch roof.

cantilever — a projecting beam or part of a structure supported only at one end.

capital — the top decorated member of a column or pilaster crowning the shaft and supporting the entablature.

cartouche — an ornamental panel in the form of a scroll, circle or oval, often bearing an inscription.

chamfer — an oblique surface produced by beveling an edge or corner, usually at a 45° angle.

choragic monument — in ancient Greece, a commemorative structure, erected by the successful leader in the competitive choral dances in a Dionysiac festival, upon which was displayed the bronze tripod received as a prize; such monuments sometimes were further ornamented by renowned artists.

clapboard — a long, narrow board with one edge thicker than the other, overlapped to cover the outer walls of frame structures; also known as weatherboard.

clerestory — the upper part of the nave, transepts, and choir of a church containing windows; also, any similar windowed wall or construction used for light and ventilation.

coffering — ceiling with deeply recessed panels, often highly ornamented.

Composite order — one of the five classical orders. A Roman elaboration of the Corinthian order, having the acanthus leaves of its capital combined with the large volutes of the Ionic order, and other details also elaborated.

console — a bracket-like member used to support a cornice of a lintel or for an ornament as the keystone of an arch.

corbel — a bracket or block projecting from the face of a wall that generally supports a cornice, beam, or arch.

Corinthian order — the most ornate of the classical Greek orders of architecture, characterized by a slender fluted column with a bell-shaped capital decorated with stylized acanthus leaves; variations of this order were extensively used by the Romans.

cornice — the top member of the entablature or any similar projecting moldings used above openings or at the top of a wall.

crenellation — a battlement.

cyma recta — a molding of double curvature which is concave at the outer edge and convex at the inner edge.

denticulated — provided with dentils, small rectangular blocks in a series, projecting like teeth from the cornice of a classic order of architecture.

distyle-in-antis — an arrangement of two columns between antae, this forming a recessed portal or portico.

Doric order — the oldest and simplest of the classical Greek orders, characterized by heavy fluted columns with no base, plain saucer-shaped capitals and a bold simple cornice.

dormer — a vertically set window on a sloping roof; also, the roofed structure housing such a window.

double-hung sash window — a window with two sash, one above the other, arranged to slide vertically past each other.

eaves — the projecting overhang at the lower edge of a roof.

egg-and-dart — a decorative molding comprised of alternating egg-shaped and dart-shaped motifs.

entablature — a system of moldings crowning the columns of a classic order of architecture. It consists of three well-defined bands: the architrave, the frieze, and the cornice.

entasis — the swell or curve in the shaft of a column to correct a hollowing optical effect.

fanlight — a semicircular or fan-shaped window with radiating members of tracery set over a door or window.

fascia — any long, flat surface of wood, stone, or marble, especially in the Ionic and Corinthian orders, each of the three surfaces which make up the architrave.

fenestration — the arrangement and proportioning of windows; hence the adornment of an architectural composition by means of window (or door) openings.

festoon — a wreath or garland of flowers, leaves, paper, cloth, etc. hanging in a loop or curve, or any carved or molded decoration resembling this.

finial — an ornament at the top of a spire, gable, pinnacle.

flutes or fluting — the grooves or channels on the shaft of a classic column.

foliated — decorated with leaf ornamentation of a design comprised of arcs or lobes.

fractable — a coping on the gable wall of a building, when carried above the roof.

frieze — that band of the entablature between the architrave and the cornice. It is a flat member, either plain or ornamented with triglyphs or bas-relief; any ornamental band, as on a wall.

gambrel — a ridged roof with two slopes on each side, the lower slope having the steeper pitch.

gutta — one of a series of pendant ornaments, generally in the form of the frustum of a cone, but sometimes cylindrical; usually found on the underside of the mutules and regulae of Doric entablatures.

hipped roof — a roof with four uniformly pitched sides.

hood molding — a large molding over a window, originally designed to direct water away from the wall; also called a drip molding.

Ionic order — an order of classical Greek architecture, characterized by a capital with two opposed volutes.

kerf — the decorative form or knob as left by the cut base of a branch.

lancet — a narrow pointed arch.

lantern — a structure built on the top of a roof with open or windowed walls.

leaded glass — small panes of glass which are held in place with lead strips; the glass may be clear or stained.

lintel — a horizontal structural member over an opening which carries the weight of the wall above it.

lunette — a crescent-shaped or semicircular area on a wall or vaulted ceiling, framed by an arch or vault.

mansard roof — a roof having a double slope on all four sides, the lower slope being much steeper. (Named for Francois Mansard 1598–1666)

modillion — a horizontal bracket or console, usually in the form of a scroll with acanthus, supporting the corona under a cornice.

mullion — a vertical bar dividing the lights in a window, especially in Gothic architecture; also, a similar bar in screen-work.

muntin — a central vertical piece between two panels, the side pieces being called stiles.

ogee — a double curve, formed by the union of a convex and concave line, resembling an S-shape.

Palladian window — a window grouping consisting of a circular-headed opening, flanked by lower square-headed openings, popularized by the Italian architect, Andrea Palladio, in the sixteenth century.

palmette, palmate — ornament derived from a palm leaf.

pediment — the triangular space forming the gable of a classic building; hence a similar form used above porticoes, doors, windows, etc.

pendant — a suspended feature or hanging ornament.

pilaster — a shallow pier attached to a wall, often decorated to resemble a classical column.

portico — a major porch, usually with a pedimented roof supported by classical columns.

quoin — a masonry block used to define and ornament the exterior angles of a building; sometimes simulated in wooden architecture.

reeding — an ornament of adjacent, parallel, protruding, half-round moldings.

reveal — the vertical side of a door or window opening between the frame and the wall surface.

rosette — stylized floral decoration.

roundel — a decorative panel, plate, medallion, etc., of a round form.

rustication — masonry cut in massive blocks separated from each other by deep joints.

standing seam — a joint in a metal roof formed by folding so that the cut edges may be covered by a fold.

stencil — a thin sheet of metal, cardboard, etc., in which one or more holes have been cut, of such shape that when a brush charged with pigment is passed over the back of the sheet, a desired pattern, letter, or figure is produced upon the surface upon which the sheet is laid.

swag — a festoon in which the object suspended resembles a piece of draped cloth.

tetrastyle — an adjective describing a classic portico with four columns.

Tower of the Winds — octagonal marble Tower of the Winds in Athens, a water clock constructed in the first century B.C. by Androcicus Cyrrhestes. (Giovanni Becatti, *The Art of Ancient Greece and Rome*)

trabeated — an adjective describing a structure designed upon the post- (or column-) and-lintel principle, not arcuate.

tracery — the curved mullions of a stone-framed window; also, ornamental work or pierced patterns in or on a screen, window glass, or panel.

trefoil — a design of three lobes, similar to a cloverleaf.

triglyph — a member or ornament in the Doric order, consisting of a block or a tablet with three vertical grooves or glyphs (strictly, two whole grooves, and a half-groove on each side), repeated at regular intervals along the frieze, usually one over each column, and one or two between every two columns.

tympanum — the recessed face of a pediment, usually triangular; it may be plain or ornamented by bas-relief or openings.

volute — a spiral scroll-like ornament.

water leaf — 1. in early Roman and Greek ornamentation, a type of lotus leaf... 2. similar to water leaf 1 but divided symmetrically by a prominent rib.

weatherboard — clapboard; wooden siding.

Definitions for the terms in this glossary have been taken from the following sources:

Cyril M. Harris, ed. *Illustrated Dictionary of Historic Architecture*. New York: Dover, 1983. (Originally published: *Historic Architecture Sourcebook*. New York: McGraw-Hill, 1977.)

Rexford Newcomb. *Architecture of the Old Northwest Territory*. Chicago: University of Chicago Press, 1950.

Oxford Universal Dictionary on Historical Principles. Third Edition Revised. Oxford: Clarendon Press, 1955.

John Poppeliers. *What Style Is It?* Washington: The Preservation Press, 1977.

Webster's New World Dictionary of the American Language. College Edition. Cleveland and New York: World Publishing Company, 1960.

Bibliography

Books

Andrews, Wayne. *Architecture, Ambition, and Americans: A Social History of American Architecture.* rev. ed. New York: Free Press, 1978.

Audsley, W. and Audsley, G. *Designs and Patterns from Historic Ornament.* New York: Dover, 1968. Originally published as *Outlines of Ornament in the Leading Styles* in 1882.

Badger, Daniel D. *Illustrated Catalogue of Cast-Iron Architecture.* New York: Dover, 1981. First published in 1865 under the title *Illustrations of Iron Architecture Made by the Architectural Iron Works of the City of New York.*

Benjamin, Asher. *The American Builder's Companion: or, A System of Architecture Particularly Adapted to the Present Style of Building.* New York: Dover, 1969. An unabridged reprint of the sixth edition with seventy plates and a new introduction by William Morgan.

———. *The Builder's Guide, Illustrated by Sixty-six Engravings, Which Exhibit the Orders of Architecture and Other Elements of the Art: Designed for the Use of Builders, Particularly of Carpenters and Joiners.* Boston: Perkins and Marvin; Philadelphia: Henry Perkins, 1839.

Biddle, Owen. *The Young Carpenter's Assistant; or a System of Architecture Adapted to the Style of Building in the United States.* Philadelphia: Johnson and Warner, 1810.

Bullock, Orin M., Jr. *The Restoration Manual: An Illustrated Guide to the Preservation and Restoration of Old Buildings.* Norwalk, Conn.: Silvermine Publishers, Inc., 1966.

Burns, Lee. *Early Architects and Builders of Indiana.* Indiana Historical Society Publications, vol. 11, no. 3. Indianapolis: Indiana Historical Society, 1935.

The Charter of the City of Madison Passed by the General Assembly of the State of Indiana, at the Session of 1837–8, and Amendments Thereto, Passed 1838–9 and 1844–5, Together with the Ordinances and Resolutions of the City Council. Madison, 1846.

Clark, Kenneth. *The Gothic Revival: An Essay in the History of Taste.* London, England: Murray, 1962.

Davidson, Marshall B. *The American Heritage History of Notable American Houses.* New York: American Heritage Pub. Co., 1971.

Downing, Andrew Jackson. *The Architecture of Country Houses.* New York: Da Capo Press, 1968. "The ninth time...republished since it first appeared in 1850" (Introduction).

———. *Cottage Residences, Rural Architecture & Landscape Gardening.* Library of Victorian Culture, 1967.

Drury, John. *Historic Midwest Houses.* Minneapolis: University of Minnesota Press, 1947.

Eastlake, Charles Locke. *History of the Gothic Revival.* Leicester University Press; Humanities Press, 1872.

Fitch, James Marston. *American Building: The Historical Forces That Shaped It.* 2d rev. ed. Boston: Houghton Mifflin, 1966.

Fowler, Orson S. *The Octagon House, a Home for All.* New York: Dover, 1970. An unabridged republication of the work originally published in 1853 by Fowler and Wells under the title *A Home for All, or The Gravel Wall and Octagon Mode of Building.*

Gillon, Edmund V., Jr., and Lancaster, Clay. *Victorian Houses: A Treasury of Lesser-Known Examples.* New York: Dover, 1973.

Goldfield, David R. and Brownell, Blaine A. *Urban America: From Downtown to No Town.* Boston: Houghton Mifflin, 1979.

Hamlin, Talbot. *Benjamin Henry Latrobe.* New York: Oxford University Press, 1955.

————. *Greek Revival Architecture in America: Being an Account of Important Trends in American Architecture and American Life Prior to the War between the States.* New York: Dover, 1964.

Handlin, David P. *The American Home Architecture and Society, 1815–1915.* Boston: Little, Brown and Co., 1979.

Harris, Cyril M., ed. *Dictionary of Architecture and Construction.* New York: McGraw-Hill, 1975.

————.ed. *Illustrated Dictionary of Historic Architecture.* New York: Dover, 1983. Originally published by McGraw-Hill in 1977 under the title *Historic Architecture Sourcebook.*

Karp, Ben. *Ornamental Carpentry on Nineteenth-Century American Houses.* New York: Dover, 1981. This Dover edition is a revised edition of the work originally published in 1966 by A. S. Barnes and Co. with the title *Wood Motifs in American Domestic Architecture.*

Kimball, Fiske. *American Architecture.* Indianapolis: Bobbs-Merrill, 1928.

Koeper, Frederick. *Illinois Architecture: From Territorial Times to the Present, A Selective Guide.* Chicago: University of Chicago Press, 1968.

Lafever, Minard. *The Architectural Instructor, Containing a History of Architecture from the Earliest Ages to the Present Time....* New York: G. P. Putnam, 1856.

————. *The Beauties of Modern Architecture.* Da Capo Press Series in Architecture and Decorative Art, vol. 18. New York: Da Capo Press, 1968. An unabridged republication of the first edition published in New York in 1835.

————. *The Modern Builder's Guide.* New York: Dover, 1969. A reprint of the first (1833) edition with three additional plates from the third edition.

————. *The Modern Practice of Staircase and Handrail Construction, Practically Explained, in a Series of Designs...with Plans and Elevations for Ornamental Villas.* New York: D. Appleton and Co., 1838.

————. *The Young Builder's General Instructor, Containing the Five Orders of Architecture....* Newark, N.J.: Tuttle and Co., 1829.

Lingeman, Richard. *Small Town America: A Narrative History 1620-The Present.* New York: G. P. Putnam, 1980.

Loth, Calder and Sadle, Julius Trousdale, Jr. *The Only Proper Style.* Boston: New York Graphic Society, 1975.

Madison City Directory, 1859–60, 1867, 1871–72, 1872–73, 1875, 1879, 1887–88, 1890–91, 1903, 1909, 1912, 1923, 1927, 1936, 1939, 1942, 1947.

Madison's 175th Anniversary, 1809–1984: Official Commemorative Book for the Dodrasquicentennial of Madison, Indiana. Madison, 1984.

Newcomb, Rexford. *Architecture in Old Kentucky*. Urbana, Illinois: University of Illinois Press, 1953.

———.*Architecture of the Old Northwest Territory: A Study of Early Architecture in Ohio, Indiana, Illinois, Michigan, Wisconsin & Part of Minnesota*. Chicago: University of Chicago Press, 1950.

———.*Outlines of the History of Architecture, Part IV: Modern Architecture with Particular Reference to the United States*. New York: John Wiley and Sons, 1939.

Newton, Roger Hale. *Town and Davis, Architects*. New York: Columbia University, 1942.

Peat, Wilbur. *Indiana Houses of the Nineteenth Century*. Indianapolis: Indiana Historical Society, 1962.

Pierce, William H., Jr. *American Buildings and Their Architects: The Colonial and Neo-classical Styles*. American Buildings and Their Architects, vol 1. Garden City, N.Y.: Doubleday, 1970.

Poppeliers, John, Chambers, S. Allen, and Schwartz, Nancy B. *What Style Is It?* Washington, D. C.: The Preservation Press of the National Trust for Historic Preservation, 1977. Reprinted from *Historic Preservation*, the magazine of the National Trust.

Pratt, Dorothy, and Pratt, Richard. *A Guide to Early American Homes — North*. New York: McGraw-Hill, 1956.

Refkind, Carole. *Main Street. The Face of Urban America*. New York: Harper and Row, 1977.

Roth, Leland M. *A Concise History of American Architecture*. New York: Harper and Row, 1979.

Sheraton, Thomas. *The Cabinet-Maker and Upholsterer's Drawing-Book*. New York: Dover, 1972. "This Dover edition reproduces material from various early editions of *The Cabinet-Maker and Upholsterer's Drawing-Book* published by the author in London between 1793 and 1802."

Sirkis, Nancy. *Reflections of 1776: The Colonies Revisited*. New York: Viking, 1974.

Skjelver, Mabel Cooper. *Nineteenth Century Homes of Marshall, Michigan*. Marshall, Mich.: Marshall Historical Society, 1977.

Slade, Thomas M. *Historic American Buildings Survey in Indiana*. Bloomington, Ind.: Indiana University Press, 1983.

Smith, Dwight L. *Goodly Heritage: One Hundred Fifty Years of Craft Freemasonry in Indiana*. n.p., n.p., 1968.

Smith, G. E. Kidder. *A Pictorial History of Architecture in America*. 2 vols. New York: American Heritage Pub. Co., 1976.

Vaux, Calvert. *Villas and Cottages*. New York: Da Capo Press, 1968. "An unabridged republication of the first edition published in New York in 1857 by Harper and Brothers."

Walsh, Charles F., comp. *St. Michael's Church, Madison, Indiana: A Pioneer Parish of Southern Indiana, 1817–1937*. n.p., n.p., 1937. "A study in Indiana Catholic and Civil History compiled and edited by Father C. F. Walsh. The text written by Thomas P. Conry...as a Thesis submitted to the Faculty of the School of History of Loyola University, Chicago, in partial fulfillment of the requirements for the Degree of Master of Arts."

Walsh, Margaret. *The Rise of the Midwestern Meat Packing Industry*. Lexington, Ky.: University of Kentucky Press, 1982.

Walters, Betty Lawson. *Furniture Makers of Indiana, 1793 to 1850*. Indiana Historical Society Publications, vol. 25, no. 1. Indianapolis: Indiana Historical Society, 1972.

The Way It Was: Glimpses into the Past of Madison and Jefferson County. Madison, 1975.

Whiffen, Marcus. *American Architecture Since 1780: A Guide to the Styles*. Cambridge, Mass.: M.I.T. Press, 1969.

Williams, Henry Lionel, and Williams, Ottalie K. *Old American Houses, 1700–1850: How to Restore, Remodel, and Reproduce Them*. New York: Coward-McCann, 1957.

Zimmer, Donald T. "The Ohio River: Pathway to Settlement." In *Transportation and the Early Nation*. Indianapolis: Indiana Historical Society, 1982.

Newspapers

Heberhart, Charles E. "They Say and Do in the Country," Madison *Courier*, 18 May 1938–14 October 1940. This is a running title used by Heberhart for a series that he wrote for newspapers.

Liberty Hall (Cincinnati)

Madison *Courier*, 30 September 1937, 10 November 1939

Madison *Courier and Constitutional Advocate*

Madison *Daily Courier*

Madison *Daily Evening Courier*

Madison *Daily Evening Star*

Madison *Daily Madisonian*

Madison *Daily Tribune*

Madison *Indiana Republican*

Madison *Republican and Banner*

Madison *Republican Banner*

Madison *Weekly Citizen*

Madison *Weekly Courier*

Madison *Weekly Herald*

Magazines

"The Editor's Attic: David Wilson — Midwestern Cabinet-Maker," *Antiques*, vol. 48, no. 4, October 1945, p. 138.

"The Oldest Miller in America," *The Millstone*, March 1882, p. 1.

Visher, Stephen S., "The Location of Indiana Towns and Cities," *Indiana Magazine of History*, 51 (1955): 341–46.

Pamphlets

St. Michael's Church, Madison, Indiana. n.p., n.p., n.d.

Tri-Kappa Tour of Historic Homes, 1950, 1951, 1953, 1954, 1956, 1958, 1960, 1962, 1964, 1966, 1968, 1970, 1972, 1974, 1976, 1978, 1980, 1982, 1984.

Unpublished Sources

Indianapolis, Indiana. Indiana Division, Indiana State Library. Robert J. Elvin scrapbook.

Indianapolis, Indiana. Indiana Division, Indiana State Library. Sophronia S. Lewis scrapbooks.

Indianapolis, Indiana. William Henry Smith Library, Indiana Historical Society. Gertrude E. Gibson, "History of Madison Markets, 1825–1906."

Mozengo, Todd R. "Francis Costigan: A Stylistic Study." Master's thesis, University of Virginia, 1975.

Muncie, Emery O. "A History of Jefferson County, Indiana." Master's thesis, Indiana University, 1932.

U.S. Department of the Interior. Historic American Buildings Survey, IN-90, IN-92, IN-123–135. 1978.

Zimmer, Donald T. "Madison, Indiana, 1811–1860: A Study in the Process of City Building." Ph.D. dissertation, Indiana University, 1974.

Index by Street Addresses

Buildings not in Madison

Index